W9-BYK-284

REINHOLD NIEBUHR

ABINGDON PILLARS
OF THEOLOGY

Reinhold Niebuhr

Robin W. Lovin

Abingdon Press
Nashville

REINHOLD NIEBUHR

Copyright © 2007 by Abingdon Press

All rights reserved.

No part of this work may be reproduced or transmitted in any form or by any means, electronic or mechanical, including photocopying and recording, or by any information storage or retrieval system, except as may be expressly permitted by the 1976 Copyright Act or in writing from the publisher. Requests for permission should be addressed to Abingdon Press, P.O. Box 801, 201 Eighth Avenue South, Nashville, TN 37202-0801 or permissions@abingdonpress.com.

This book is printed on acid-free paper.

Library of Congress Cataloging-in-Publication Data

Lovin, Robin W.
  Reinhold Niebuhr / Robin W. Lovin.
    p. cm.—(Abingdon pillars of theology)
  Includes bibliographical references and index.
  ISBN 978-0-687-64612-8 (binding: pbk., : alk. paper)
  1. Niebuhr, Reinhold, 1892–1971.   I. Title.

BX4827.N5L67 2007
230.092—dc22

2007005628

All scripture quotations unless noted otherwise are taken from the HOLY BIBLE: NEW INTERNATIONAL VERSION®. Copyright © 1973, 1978, 1984 by the International Bible Society. Used by permission of Zondervan Publishing House. All rights reserved.

Scripture quotations marked (CEV) are from the Contemporary English Version, © 1991, 1992, 1995 by American Bible Society. Used by permission.

Scripture quotations marked (KJV) are from the King James or Authorized Version of the Bible.

Scripture quotations marked (NRSV) are taken from the *New Revised Standard Version of the Bible,* copyright 1989, Division of Christian Education of the National Council of the Churches of Christ in the United States of America. Used by permission. All rights reserved.

Scripture quotations marked (RSV) are taken from the Revised Standard Version of the Bible, copyright 1946, 1952, 1971 by the Division of Christian Education of the National Council of the Churches of Christ in the United States of America. Used by permission. All rights reserved.

Portions of chapter 6 were first published in Robin W. Lovin, "Christian Realism: A Legacy and Its Future," *The Annual of the Society of Christian Ethics* (Decatur, Ga.: Society of Christian Ethics, 2000): 3–18.

Portions of chapter 6 were first published in Robin W. Lovin, "Reinhold Niebuhr: Impact and Implications," *Political Theology* 6, no. 4 (2005): 459–71. Copyright © 2005 by Equinox Publishing Ltd.

07 08 09 10 11 12 13 14 15 16—10 9 8 7 6 5 4 3 2 1

MANUFACTURED IN THE UNITED STATES OF AMERICA

CONTENTS

PREFACE

Reinhold Niebuhr had an enormous influence on twentieth-century theologians and on the public perception of theology. This was true not only for the generation who read his books and heard his sermons but also for subsequent students, pastors, and public leaders who have absorbed his ideas indirectly, sometimes without knowing it, and sometimes through the works of his critics. In this book, I hope to introduce Reinhold Niebuhr and his Christian realism to new readers who will make use of his ideas in a different historical and social context.

I have been encouraged in this by the warm reception these reflections have received in many church classes and study groups in Dallas, especially in an interfaith seminar at Thanksgiving Square and in my own congregation at Northaven United Methodist Church. I have also drawn on material from previously published lectures, especially for the last chapter of this book. "Christian Realism: A Legacy and Its Future" was my presidential address to the Society of Christian Ethics in 2000. It appeared in *The Annual of the Society of Christian Ethics* (Decatur, Ga.: Society of Christian Ethics, 2000): 3–18. "Reinhold Niebuhr: Impact and Implications" began as a lecture to the Niebuhr Society in November 2004. It appeared in *Political Theology* 6, no. 4 (2005): 459–71.

Although I have discussed Niebuhr in almost every course I have taught over thirty years, I had never devoted a full semester exclusively to his work until spring 2006 at Perkins School of Theology of Southern Methodist University. The experience made me sorry I had not done this more often, though I suppose that it was the ability of those students, rather than my handling of the material, that made the seminar exceptional.

Oleg Makariev, my research assistant, improved these pages with his meticulous editing and prodigious memory, as he has improved most of my writing during these past four years. John Burk prepared the selected bibliography at the end of the book, and Stephen Riley checked the notes.

INTRODUCTION

Living the Christian life is not easy. It involves a high standard of righteousness learned from an ancient text, but lived in contemporary circumstances. It presupposes we will fall short of the requirements, but insists that we measure our accomplishments against that standard nonetheless. In the end, the Christian trusts in God's final judgment, even though the evidence of history is ambiguous and the immediate advantage often seems to lie with power and not with goodness.

Reinhold Niebuhr understood these tensions and complexities. He saw the teachings of Jesus rooted in the tradition of the Hebrew prophets. Because this prophetic justice requires more of us than we can ever deliver, we inevitably choose what part of this "impossible ideal" we will try to live today, and we leave the rest of it to stand in judgment on our best efforts. Bearing witness to so many different audiences, we inevitably speak truth to some at the price of being misunderstood by others. We appear "as deceivers, yet true." [1] We say we act with God's final judgment in mind, but we commit what we do to a future that we cannot control and can only partly predict. The moral choices of which we would like to be most certain are, when we examine them, always ambiguous.

Nevertheless, Niebuhr's ambiguity is in service of Christian faith, and the uncertainty is meant to provoke us to action. Indeed, prophetic faith and moral action would be impossible without ambiguity and uncertainty:

> The dominant attitudes of prophetic faith are gratitude and contrition; gratitude for Creation and contrition before Judgment; or, in other words, confidence that life is good in spite of its evil and that it is evil in spite of its good. In such a faith both sentimentality and despair are avoided. The meaningfulness of life does not tempt to premature complacency, and the chaos which always threatens the world of meaning does not destroy the tension of faith and hope in which all moral action is grounded. [2]

Niebuhr gave the name of "Christian realism" to this approach to theology, which begins with the obstacles to faith and charts its course by identifying the inadequate and mistaken views it must reject or move beyond. This negative, dialectical method set Niebuhr in opposition to much of the received wisdom of his time, yet he came to represent active, living Christian faith for many of his contemporaries, both in the church and in the worlds of politics and diplomacy.

Niebuhr was so deeply engaged with the issues of his time that his thought cannot really be separated from the events and movements to which he responded. His active life, which spanned two-thirds of the twentieth century, brought him into contact with many religious, cultural, and political leaders, and his immense output of books, articles, and lectures influenced people far beyond his immediate circle of students and colleagues. [3] The development of his thought traces the history that he lived.

Reinhold Niebuhr was born just west of Saint Louis, Missouri, in 1892. His parents, Lydia and Gustav Niebuhr, lived their married life in a series of parsonages of the German congregations that Gustav served as pastor, culminating in a move to Saint John's Evangelical Church in Lincoln, Illinois, in 1902. This typical Midwestern town became home to Reinhold, two older children, Walter and Hulda, and his younger brother, Helmut Richard.

Three of the children in this remarkable family were drawn to vocations in theology and ministry. Hulda Niebuhr became a professor of Christian education at McCormick Theological Seminary in Chicago. Reinhold and H. Richard followed the Evangelical Synod's path toward ministry by studying at Elmhurst College and at Eden Theological Seminary, and both completed further studies at Yale Divinity School. [4]

Reinhold briefly served the congregation in Lincoln, Illinois, following his father's unexpected death in 1913, but his career began in earnest after his two years at Yale, when he became pastor of a small congregation of middle-class German-Americans in Detroit. The industrial city was a mirror of America's economic and social problems at the beginning of the twentieth century, and Niebuhr became involved in most of them. He invited union organizers to speak to his congregation, and he served on a city commission organized to improve relations after a race riot in 1925.

Despite his prominence in Detroit, his vision was never strictly local. He began to write widely about problems of church and society for *The Christian Century* and other publications. He wrote about national politics, traveled in Germany and Russia, and published a memoir of his years as a pastor, writer, and church leader. [5] The first three decades of the twentieth century took Reinhold Niebuhr far from his small-town background. They took America far from the optimism and religious idealism with which the new century had begun.

When Niebuhr left Detroit to join the faculty of Union Theological Seminary in 1928, his mood and the temper of the times were more focused on the obstacles to peace and justice than on the possibilities for social transformation. The sentimental pieties of American Protestantism were confronting the realities of class and racial conflict at home, Europe on the edge of revolution, and the first stirrings of resistance to colonialism in India. It was becoming harder to imagine that Christian love and American energy could change the world in ways that the typical Sunday morning sermon urged the congregation to believe.

In 1932, Niebuhr published his first major book, *Moral Man and Immoral Society*, in an effort to change Christian thinking so that it could deal with these new realities. Social institutions are shaped by self-interest and power, he explained, and while individuals may sometimes make sacrifices out of love for their families, friends, or even for their country, groups will never do this. Societies are transformed by people who know how to use power to force change. Exhortations to love are beside the point, and though revolutionaries may dream of perfect justice, the changes they actually bring about will be limited, imperfect, and incomplete. [6] Once Christians understand that—once they "stop fooling themselves," as Niebuhr put it, they will devise more realistic plans for mission and ministry.

The Sermon on the Mount and Jesus' commandment to love our neighbors as ourselves cannot provide a blueprint for society. The function of Jesus' teaching is more to remind us of the limitations of all the high-minded plans we make in Jesus' name or in cooperation with others who think that we can achieve justice if only we set our sights high enough. Responsible choices achieve limited goals, without claiming too much for their achievements and without denying the element of self-interest that remains in even our most moral actions. "Human happiness ... is determined by the difference between a little more and a little less justice, a little more and a little less freedom, between varying degrees of imaginative insight with which the self enters the life and understands the interests of the neighbour." [7]

It is this realism about Christian aspirations and social forces that we will explore in chapter 1 of this book. Precisely because Niebuhr's influence on subsequent theology and ethics has made his ideas so familiar, we need to remember that this was a shocking renunciation of the idealism of many of his contemporaries. *Moral Man and Immoral Society* led even some of Niebuhr's friends and colleagues to suspect that he had abandoned religious hope and taken up a secular view of history and human society. Their suspicions were furthered, no doubt, by the strong influence of Marxism in Niebuhr's understanding of social conflict, although he also criticized the illusions that the Marxists had about their own ability to create a new and lasting social order.

Niebuhr himself was clear that his realism was a *Christian* realism. His awareness of human limitations and his suspicion of power drew on the Hebrew prophets. His insistence that Jesus' commandments are impossible to follow reflected his belief in a Christ whose significance for human history could not be reduced to the wise sayings of a moral teacher. These theological affirmations were apparent in his preaching from the beginning, but during the 1930s, they became more evident in his systematic thinking about ethics and politics. The political and economic crises that swept Europe and America had to be understood in ways that transcended their immediate historical context. With the Western democracies preparing for war against Nazi totalitarianism in Germany and keeping a wary eye on Stalinist dictatorship in the Soviet Union, Niebuhr believed that only a view that could interpret the clash of ideologies and the threats to peace in light of a comprehensive, biblical understanding of human nature would be adequate to the times.

Niebuhr developed his most systematic treatment of Christian theology and ethics in two series of Gifford Lectures, which were delivered in Edinburgh, Scotland, in 1939, and published as *The Nature and Destiny of Man.* [8] Between the spring and fall lectures, Hitler attacked Poland, and Britain went to war with Germany in September. At one lecture in October, Niebuhr's audience could hear sounds of an air attack on the naval yards a few miles away. [9] By that point, the emphasis on power and self-interest that had seemed so pessimistic in 1932 fit the realities very well, and Niebuhr's theological analysis, which found the results of human sin both in the ambitions of dictators and in the failures of peacemakers, made sense of events in ways that purely political and economic explanations could not.

It was the emphasis on sin that Niebuhr's audience and subsequent readers remembered best. In the biblical understanding, a person is both "created in the image of God" and created in finite, limited humanity. Sin is a not a mistake that we might avoid by being more careful about what we do. It is a deliberate misuse of the freedom that is our image of God in an effort to deny the reality of our human limitations. [10] Sin is a self-contradiction in which humanity destroys the very freedom that it seeks to demonstrate when it claims power over others and tries to impose its own will on circumstances. For a generation of theologians and political thinkers, this attentiveness to self-interest and power and to the hold they have on the behavior of individuals and nations defined a realistic approach to politics. Idealistic appeals to Christian love offered little help in understanding the events that led up to the Second World War or the Cold War that followed it, but Niebuhr's demonstration that the paradoxes of human nature shape politics as profoundly as they shape individual lives won acceptance from theologians, political theorists, and political activists alike.

Niebuhr's theology was not limited to an analysis of human evil, however. He also sought to understand how people find meaning in a world where they are so often crushed by the evil done by others or defeated by their own illusions of goodness. He could not share an earlier generation's confidence in human progress, but he did not think that a purely tragic view of life was compatible with the biblical understanding, either. Human destiny, viewed in light of faith that God will prevail over the failures and reverses of history, is as important to Niebuhr's understanding of theology and ethics as his account of human nature, though it has not received as much attention from those who have studied Niebuhr's thought and made practical use of his ideas. In this book, we will focus on human nature in chapter 2 and human destiny in chapter 3, but we will try to see them in the close connection that they had for Niebuhr himself, rather than distinct, as they have sometimes become.

Human destiny is important because it motivates our commitment to concrete, specific actions in history, just as human nature keeps us from claiming too much for them. Without an understanding of sin, we might think that we were authorized by God to fulfill human destiny by imposing God's will on our recalcitrant neighbors or on reluctant nations. But without an understanding of human destiny, we might despair of achieving anything, watching our best efforts swallowed up in the effects of sin. The despair is not lightened by the recognition that often the sin is our own. What human nature and human destiny together require is *responsible* action that recognizes the limitations of self-interest and imperfect understanding in everything we do, but also understands the importance of the choices we make within those limitations. "We are men, not God," Niebuhr wrote. "We are responsible for making choices between greater and lesser evils, even when our Christian faith, illuminating the human scene, makes it quite apparent that there is no pure good in history; and probably no pure evil, either. The fate of civilizations may depend upon these choices of which some are more, others less, just." [11]

During and after the Second World War, Niebuhr's thought moved more to these problems of responsible choice, to ethics rather than theology. He wanted to understand how responsible politics could take the form of a commitment to democracy, and he wanted at the same time to warn the leaders of democratic nations that expecting too much from their own wisdom would lead them into the same overconfidence that had destroyed their totalitarian opponents. In a world shaped by two imperial powers, the United States and the Soviet Union, democracy had the difficult task of maintaining enough power to counterbalance the external threat without succumbing to temptations to use that power in ways that might ultimately destroy democratic freedom. [12] Niebuhr's ideas found a wide following among the political leaders and policy makers who shaped postwar America, and the defense of democracy in his writings during these years is his most complete statement of the practical implications of Christian realism, though the theological ideas on which the system depends are no longer in the foreground. This book focuses on Niebuhr's understanding of democracy in chapter 4.

In the postwar years, Niebuhr often seems a figure larger than life—certainly more imposing than most theologians before or since! He was committed to his students and his classes at Union Theological Seminary. He gave leadership in practical political organizations like Americans for Democratic Action, and he participated in theoretical discussions with philosophers and political scientists at the Center for the Study of Democratic Institutions. He maintained correspondence with leading writers, journalists, and artists, and he produced a torrent of books and articles, along with the sermons and public lectures that he delivered nearly every week. *Time* magazine featured his portrait on the cover of its twenty-fifth anniversary issue in 1948, and in the course of preparing a Sunday worship service for the congregation near his summer home in Massachusetts, he wrote what has become known to millions as the "Serenity Prayer." [13]

It is important to remember, however, that while Niebuhr achieved distinctions that few of his theological contemporaries could claim, he did not work in isolation. Much of the energy and direction in his work came from arguments with theologians who understood the relationship between theology and ethics in different terms. Karl Barth made sharper distinctions than Niebuhr did between God's commands and responsible human choices, and while Niebuhr was shaping a realistic approach to the Cold War balance of power among the politicians, many Christian leaders were pursuing a very different approach to global politics through the United Nations and the adoption of the Universal Declaration of Human Rights. Niebuhr's understanding of politics relied heavily on Luther and a Protestant understanding of sin, which led to some extended conversations with Catholic and Jewish interlocutors who had different readings of the biblical tradition. In chapter 5, we will consider some of the ways these dialogues shaped Niebuhr's Christian realism.

During Niebuhr's later years, the dominant issues of the day shifted again, from global politics and the defense of democracy to questions about justice, race, and poverty at home. The Supreme Court began the desegregation of public schools in 1954, and the 1955–1956 bus boycott in Montgomery, Alabama, launched a mass movement for civil rights that culminated in the March on Washington and the Civil Rights Act of 1964. Niebuhr had anticipated the need for this kind of mass movement as early as *Moral Man and Immoral Society*, but when the demands for change began to accelerate, he also worried that it might provoke resistance that would destroy the movement before it could achieve its goals. The contrast between Niebuhr's caution and the rising anger of younger African American leaders alienated many of them from Christian realism and led to a new Black Liberation Theology that defined itself against the established power structures with which Niebuhr was now identified. At the same time, a new feminist theology challenged Niebuhr's understanding of human nature, which gave so much attention to the sin of pride and worried so little about the spiritual effects of submission and subservience. By the time of Niebuhr's death in 1971, some new voices in theology and politics dismissed his realism as little more than an excuse for resisting inevitable changes. Not all of these criticisms were fair, and subsequent events have sometimes made Niebuhr's caution seem wiser than it did at the time, but the new movements changed the contours of theological discussion, and no assessment of Niebuhr's relevance for theology today can ignore the issues they raised.

By the beginning of the twenty-first century, many of the defining features of Reinhold Niebuhr's world had disappeared. The economic and racial divisions discussed in *Moral Man and Immoral Society* remain, but they must now be considered in global terms. Fears that our civilization might perish in a future nuclear war have given way to concern that human activity may already have initiated irreversible climate changes. The United States and Russia worry less about the threats they pose to each other and more about the ways that each of them is vulnerable to terrorist attacks or insurgent movements whose origins cannot even be clearly identified. All of these changes raise questions about political and religious ideas formed for other times, but the major themes of Niebuhr's Christian realism—the limits of human power, the distortions of self-interest, and the necessity of conflict in any genuine search for justice—often seem essential to orient ourselves to these new realities. Our final chapter will consider the legacy of Niebuhr's thought and assess its relevance for our time.

IMMORAL SOCIETY

Reinhold Niebuhr's pastoral career began in 1915, just as Europe plunged itself into the First World War. Despite initial efforts by many Americans to treat the conflict as a distant matter that did not concern them, the war touched American interests at many points, and the United States declared war on Germany in 1917. Niebuhr was immediately caught up in the mobilization, serving as a representative of the Evangelical Synod in ministry to its young men recruited into military service and raising funds for that work. The denomination's German heritage raised some questions about its loyalty, and in response, Niebuhr became a strong voice for American patriotism in its churches.

The war raised important questions for American religion and society. Americans had believed in "progress," a steady movement toward peace, prosperity, and democracy on a global scale. Progress was often slow, but its direction was always forward, and many Americans thought that its pace had accelerated in the last half of the nineteenth century. Christianity made progress, too, according to the theologians. While a new fundamentalist movement had begun to insist on a literal reading of the Bible, a more broadly based liberal theology argued that Christian truths were compatible with new scientific knowledge and that Christian values were consistent with democracy and personal freedom. Then, with little warning, the European cradle of this progress tore itself apart in a war of unprecedented brutality and destruction. Worse still, the church leaders of the rival nations were often caught up in the same patriotic fury. The faith that claimed to be the spiritual manifestation of progress proved no more effective than its secular counterparts at resisting the forces of chaos.

In the disillusionment that followed, many repudiated all patriotic values, and many young pastors and theologians became pacifists. After a postwar trip through the occupied zone in Germany, Niebuhr repented of his wartime enthusiasm and considered embracing pacifism himself. "This is as good a time as any to make up my mind that I am done with the war business.... I hope I can make that resolution stick."[1]

Others posed more basic challenges to the identification of Christian faith and human progress. The Swiss theologian Karl Barth drew on the more enduring message of God's judgment on human sin, with a Protestant insistence that this judgment can be answered only by God's grace. Human achievements are meaningless against it.[2] With the apparent failure of Europe's social and cultural achievements since the Enlightenment, Christians began to give new attention to distinctly theological ideas in the Bible and in historic statements of their faith. Barth called this "crisis theology," drawing on a Greek word that can refer both to a time of crisis and to a moment of judgment. Others, focusing on the return to central, historic doctrines, called it "neo-orthodoxy." Its sharp distinction between the Word of God and the values of nation and culture would be an important resource a decade or so later, when Christians in Germany had to resist the new National Socialism of Adolf Hitler.

Because of his European travels and his ability to read German, Niebuhr knew Barth's work better than most American theologians at the time. He wrote an early review of Barth's work for *The Christian Century*,[3] and Barth remained an important dialogue partner, in print and in person, through the rest of his work. Niebuhr understood, however, that the American religious situation was different. American churches had less connection to the doctrines and creeds of earlier Christian orthodoxy, and they associated a return to the Bible with a fundamentalist, literal interpretation that was quite different from Barth's theology. Above all, American Christians had an evangelical, revivalist heritage that led them to think that social problems could be overcome by transformation of each individual believer's heart and life. That was the most important illusion that Christian realism had to overcome.

Toward the end of the nineteenth century, American Protestantism developed the idea of a Social Gospel to address the problems of crime and poverty in the growing industrial cities and the unrest of the workers, many of them recent immigrants, who worked in the factories, lived crowded in the slums, and often lacked access to the public education and Protestant churches that had shaped earlier generations of Americans. Christian faith required a greater concern for their welfare, and if the prosperous and powerful Christians who controlled the cities and industries would only live their faith, the poor would have opportunities to rise above their misery without violence or agitation.

This Social Gospel idea caught the popular imagination in the novel *In His Steps*, published by Charles M. Sheldon in 1897. In Sheldon's novel, a city is transformed by a congregation whose members agree for a year to ask themselves in every situation, "What would Jesus do?"[4] Under the influence of that question, employers provide education and better working conditions for their employees, earnest young Christians rescue the city's fallen women from their plight, and the city's political bosses begin to think about the community's good, rather than personal profit. Everyone stops abusing the African Americans. This sincerity and good will is, of course, appreciated and reciprocated, and as a result workers, servants, and the poor become productive, dignified members of society.

No one thought this would be quite as easy as Sheldon's novel made it appear. The Social Gospel preachers and theologians were not naïve. Many of them knew firsthand what they were up against, because they had done ministry in the crowded, disease-ridden factory districts they wanted to change. But they were confident that the combination of new social science and progressive Christianity had given them an opportunity for social improvement that had no parallel in human history. Walter Rauschenbusch, the greatest theologian of the Social Gospel, put it this way: "If the twentieth century could do for us in the control of social forces what the nineteenth did for us in the control of natural forces, our grandchildren would live in a society that would be justified in regarding our present social life as semi-barbarous." [5]

A decade later, as America entered the First World War, even Rauschenbusch had a more sober estimate of the difficulties of the situation. [6] By the 1930s, the optimism of the culture was largely gone, but Protestant clergy continued to preach the same sermons about personal faith and social transformation. What Niebuhr understood was that although the church talked a great deal about a scientific understanding of social forces, it still relied heavily on Christian idealism in its preaching and its moral teaching. If the factory owners could only be persuaded of the difference they could make, they would give up their profits to make the community better. And of course, if the industrialists did that, workers would stop striking and accept just wages, and everyone would stop discriminating against African Americans. Niebuhr's contribution was simply to insist that this was not going to happen, no matter how good the preaching got.

What was missing from these idealistic expectations was an understanding of the power of self-interest to distort social realities and keep us from acting on our moral commitments. In fact, self-interest distorts our picture of social realities so much that we confuse our moral commitments and our self-interest. No employer regards the gap between wages and profits as an expression of greed that might be overcome by a sufficient commitment to the general welfare. Profits appear as a just return on the investment of skill and capital that provides opportunities for employment and makes for a secure and prosperous society. Privileged groups, Niebuhr wrote, "identify the particular organization of society, of which they are the beneficiaries, with the peace and order of society in general and . . . appoint themselves the apostles of law and order." [7] From this perspective, it conveniently appears that justice requires the privileged to retain their status, not to surrender it.

What the new tools of social analysis and economic theory reveal, then, is not a mechanism by which Christian ideals can be put into practice. Social theory explains why prosperous Christians will invariably resist change, at least when they act as part of a large group—the whole class of employers, for instance, or the members of a dominant race, collectively. "However large the number of individual white men who do and will identify themselves completely with the Negro cause," Niebuhr observed, "the white race in America will not admit the Negro to equal rights if it is not forced to do so." [8]

Martin Luther King Jr. would write much later that he learned something important from this passage in *Moral Man and Immoral Society* about his strategy for achieving racial justice. [9] Many of Niebuhr's contemporaries, however, saw only a critic who sought to undermine their Christian hopes for personal and social transformation by the use of social theories shaped by secular and materialistic ideas about humanity. They failed to see the other way of understanding change that emerges from this analysis, one that sees genuine gains rooted in social conflict, rather than personal transformation. That was a large part of what Niebuhr would mean by "Christian realism," as he explained a couple of years later in an article that marked one of the first times he used that terminology:

> The church would do more for the cause of reconciliation if, instead of producing moral idealists who think they can establish justice, it would create religious and Christian realists who know that justice will require that some men shall contend against them. In the more privileged congregations this would mean the education of Christian laymen who understand the profound realities of the social struggle, and who therefore would not give themselves to the deception that they know what is good for their workingmen and that their philanthropies are a refutation of the worker's insistence on organization. This kind of Christian realism would understand the perennial necessity of political relationships in society, no matter how ethical ideals rise. [10]

There were many young theologians and preachers who shared Niebuhr's desire for a more realistic Christianity that would avoid the exaggerated expectations of the Social Gospel and speak to the disappointments of a generation shaken by the First World War. But Niebuhr's realism, grounded in an analysis of social forces that overwhelm individual human aspirations, seemed perhaps too realistic for them at the time.

[Niebuhr's theories about social conflict regarded economic interests as the basic divisions between people] Commitments depended less on party loyalties, regional differences, or ethnic loyalties than on whether a person worked for wages like the factory workers in Detroit's auto plants or shared the powers and privileges of the owners, professionals, and managers who formed the city's elite. In *Moral Man and Immoral Society*, the people are divided into "proletarian" and "privileged" classes. [11] Niebuhr believed that the disadvantaged position of the workers gave them a certain clarity about the forces that were at work in society. They were not susceptible to illusions about the justice of the economic system or the virtues of the people who run it. While the elite might justify their privileges with the belief that they work harder or contribute more to the general prosperity than others, the workers and the poor know better. Niebuhr's views drew heavily on Marxist social and economic theory, and his emphasis on the social insight of the proletarians anticipates what liberation theologians would say much later about the "hermeneutical privilege of the oppressed." [12] Those who suffer are in a better position to say what is really going on than those who oppress them, even if the oppressors seem to have more knowledge, more education, and more information.

Niebuhr, however, did not leave matters where the Marxists left them. If the proletarians had a clearer idea of what is going on in present social relations, they were more susceptible to illusions about what could happen after a fundamental change. Marxists expected a workers' revolution that would end the regime of privileges and establish real justice. Niebuhr thought that the result of revolution would be a new set of abuses and injustices perpetrated by the revolutionaries. Marxists have insights into existing economic and social realities that penetrate beneath the surface of political slogans and moral ideals to identify the forces that actually shape social conflict, but the Marxist goal of social harmony in a classless society has more in common with religious idealism than with scientific social analysis. A realist who wants justice will encourage the aspirations that fuel revolutionary change, "for justice cannot be approximated if the hope of its perfect realization does not generate a sublime madness in the soul." [13] Still, the realist will not expect too much from the outcome. We need people driven by the illusion of perfect justice, whether their illusions are generated by Marxist theory or by the visions of an apocalyptic faith, but it is equally important to bring their fervor under control of a realism so that even if the revolution does come, injustice will not continue in new forms.

Moral Man and Immoral Society offered a grim view of the future, especially in 1932, when the economy was in the grip of a worldwide depression and the threat of more Communist revolutions like the Russian one in 1917 loomed over Europe, and perhaps over North America, too. Whether his Christian readers viewed that prospect with fear or welcomed it with enthusiasm, Niebuhr offered them equally little hope. Nor did religion play an especially promising role in his vision of the future. It might ease the consciences of the privileged or fire the imaginations of the oppressed, but its real transformative role is limited to those aspects of personal life where we are not caught up in social forces that know nothing beyond the power of self-interest. "Political morality, in other words, is in the most uncompromising antithesis to religious morality." [14] By the end of *Moral Man and Immoral Society*, there is nothing left of the Social Gospel idealism that transforms society by selfless love applied with scientific understanding.

Perhaps it was not a time for optimism. The hopes for peace that had blossomed in 1919 withered as America withdrew from world affairs and abandoned Wilson's dream of a League of Nations. European disarmament conferences failed, and militaristic dictators took power in Italy and Germany. The Empire of Japan began its aggressive expansion across Asia, and Stalin's enforced collectivization of Soviet agriculture brought an end to any remaining hopes for the early achievement of a Communist paradise. Theologians began to question whether Christianity could offer anything to the human situation beyond the patience to bear it. H. Richard Niebuhr, writing now as a professor of theology at Yale, responded to the frantic calls of Christian activists for the church to do something about the Japanese invasion of Manchuria with the observation that there might be nothing the American church could do. "The inactivity of radical Christianity is not the inactivity of those who call evil good; it is the inaction of those who do not judge their neighbors because they cannot fool themselves into a sense of superior righteousness." [15]

In the early 1930s, Reinhold Niebuhr may have believed that the collapse of Western society was inevitable. His next book, titled *Reflections on the End of an Era*, was even more pessimistic than *Moral Man and Immoral Society*. He dedicated *Reflections on the End of an Era* to his brother, but however much he may have shared the sense of impending catastrophe, he did not share H. Richard's belief that Christians had nothing to do but repent and wait for the inevitable. One of his chief complaints, in fact, was "classical Christianity's preoccupation with the problem of sin in general." This results in "a perspective in religion which reduces all social and moral striving to a single category of 'sinfulness' and makes ethical distinctions on the historical level impossible." [16]

Niebuhr himself was by no means resigned to watching the world from such a distant perspective. He combined his teaching responsibilities at Union with a heavy travel schedule of preaching and lecturing. He wrote the two books and a steady stream of articles and reviews. He made long trips to England, Germany, and the Soviet Union for study and research. He was active in politics in the Socialist Party in New York, and even ran for the state Senate and the U.S. Congress on the Socialist ticket in 1930 and 1932. At the end of 1931, he married Ursula Keppel-Compton, an Englishwoman who had been a student at Union and who would have her own academic career as a professor at Barnard College. [17] World events might tempt Christian pacifists to despair, and Niebuhr's own social theories might predict revolution, but he was putting his own immense energy into the ongoing tasks of family life and making a difference to his students, the politics of his community, and the mission of the church.

The energy that Niebuhr himself brought to the tasks of Christian political action contrasted sharply with the disillusionment of many of his contemporaries with the whole idea of social transformation. Whether he fully understood it at the time or not, he was living what he would much later call the "responsible attitude" toward questions of politics. [18] That attitude begins with an understanding of the complexity of social issues and a critical awareness of the part that self-interest plays in everyone's assessment of the possibilities. A responsible attitude is therefore suspicious of claims for large plans that promise complete solutions, but it is not paralyzed by this awareness of ambiguity. It plunges into those concrete choices that make for small differences in daily life—a little more or a little less justice, a little more or a little less freedom—with the assurance that this is how the human moral life is lived.

Niebuhr became increasingly aware that he had to explain to Christians why they should try at all to change a world that was so resistant to their efforts and so difficult to understand. Lecturing regularly on Christian ethics perhaps made him more aware of this constructive side of his task. Perhaps even more important, these classes required him to think more explicitly about the theological sources of his ethics. Those who plunged eagerly into responsible politics were not always clear about how this related to their Christian faith. Niebuhr found it increasingly important to make that connection.

A series of lectures at Colgate-Rochester Divinity School gave him the opportunity to do this in 1934. While the lectures had been established as a memorial to Walter Rauschenbusch, Niebuhr did not address the Social Gospel directly. Instead, as he explained in the preface to the published version of the lectures, he concentrated on "an application to our own day of both the social realism and the loyalty to the Christian faith" that had marked Rauschenbusch's work. Niebuhr's idea of social realism, however, required some substantial rethinking of the liberal Christianity that Rauschenbusch had championed. Liberal Christianity tended to treat the ethics of Jesus as an example of the highest and best in ordinary moral expectations. What Jesus requires is no more than "conformity with the prudential rules of conduct which the common sense of many generations and the experience of the ages have elaborated." [19] As a result, liberal Christianity tends to think of the law of love as a simple historical possibility.

Niebuhr's realism up to this point had been devoted primarily to correcting liberal optimism about this. Christian ethics cannot be a simple matter of asking, "What would Jesus do?" What Jesus did was to offer his own life for others, without any self-interested reservations or prudential calculations of the likely results. Jesus requires an unqualified love of God and our neighbor (Matthew 22:34-40) that cuts across all existing obligations and relationships. It makes nonsense of our ordinary ways of deciding right and wrong, and the final fulfillment of his commandment "is possible only when God transmutes the present chaos of this world into its final unity." [20] Those who see the law of love as a simple historical possibility, little different from the advice we might read in the newspapers or get from a TV talk show host, have not understood it.

Niebuhr might have added that the law of love is not one of the more complex historical possibilities, either. It is not that the fulfillment of Jesus' commandment is impossible now, but will become commonplace after a socialist revolution destroys the system of interests that divide social classes from one another today. Nor will it be possible in the near future that Rauschenbusch imagined, when social science has created a world of prosperity and justice that will look back on the beginning of the twentieth century as "semi-barbarous."

The law of love belongs to a time of fulfillment beyond history, which means that nothing we can do within history, even at the extreme edges of historical change, can be anything more than an approximation that denies part of the law of love, even in the act of fulfilling part of it.

Niebuhr's criticism of liberal Christianity should by that point have become familiar to his theological critics, but he began now to pay more attention to some other Christians who might have thought that they agreed with him. Social and political radicals might have begun to understand from Niebuhr's writing that their idea of perfect justice is not what Jesus taught, but in making that message clear, he had perhaps begun to sound perilously like a version of Christian orthodoxy, which held that the law of love was not meant to be obeyed, but only to convict us of sin by the very impossibility of its requirements. The orthodoxy that Niebuhr had in mind here was deeply rooted in his own German Protestant heritage, but when he connected this view to those who are "certain that the tragedy of human life must be resolved by something more than moral achievement," [21] he perhaps also had in mind those younger theologians who, like his brother, H. Richard, were so disillusioned by events that they suggested that the most effective Christian witness would be to do nothing.

Christian realism, which had begun with a rejection of the optimism of the Social Gospel, now began to thread a narrow passage between excessive optimism and a too-consistent pessimism. The attempt to discern the realistic midpoint between those two extremes would define Niebuhr's work from this point forward.

Still, he intended this discernment to result in decision and action. He sees no grace in doing nothing. His sympathies, and indeed the whole pattern of his life, were oriented toward responsible action. Perfect justice is an illusion, but the illusion grows out of the reality that human beings have the freedom and the vision to see that things might be better than they are. Enlightenment philosophers, political reformers, and Social Gospel preachers were wrong to think that we could achieve perfection in easy, progressive steps that always moved in the same direction, but they were right about human aspirations, and often they were right about the specific steps that needed to be taken in their time. Abolishing slavery, extending the right to vote, organizing unions, and opening America's cities and factories to African Americans were the right things to do. Christians may acknowledge that sin and self-interest obscure the requirements of love, but there are plenty of cases where the requirements of justice are obvious enough. Where children lack medical care in the midst of affluent cities or workers labor in sweatshops to reduce the cost of luxury goods for consumers, something needs to be done to restore the equal dignity with which all people should be treated. It would be nonsense, Niebuhr argued, for the church to insist that nothing should be done because everyone involved is equally sinful and all the choices are imperfect in God's sight. [22]

In many cases, then, Niebuhr comes to the same political conclusions as the secularists, naturalists, and liberal theologians whose progressive illusions he criticized. There is a perception of justice and injustice that persons in the same situation tend to share, and there is a fund of moral common sense and prudential wisdom that has grown over the generations. Christians share those moral experiences, and for the most part, their moral choices will connect them with others in their neighborhoods, workplaces, and organizations.

What Niebuhr wants to avoid is not the identification of Christians with those who seek equal justice. What he wants to avoid is the identification of equal justice with the law of love:

> The absolutism and perfectionism of Jesus' love ethic sets itself uncompromisingly not only against the natural self-regarding impulses, but against the necessary prudent defences of the self, required because of the egoism of others. It does not establish a connection with the horizontal points of a political or social ethic or with the diagonals which a prudential individual ethic draws between the moral ideal and the facts of a given situation. It has only a vertical dimension between the loving will of God and the will of man. [23]

One may well ask, then, how Christians actually decide what to do, especially in those cases when the liberals, secularists, and naturalists who are their natural allies happen to disagree. If the teaching of Jesus does not provide the connection between the moral ideal and the facts of a given situation, is it possible for us to draw them anyway, at least in a tentative way, for our own time and circumstances?

Many of Niebuhr's contemporaries were greatly concerned about this question. An ecumenical gathering at Oxford in 1937, titled the "Conference on Church, Community, and State," was one of the first efforts to explore these issues on an international scale. Theologians and representatives of the churches asked how their different societies and denominations could deal as Christians with the worldwide economic crisis and the growing threat of war. They devised the concept of "middle axioms," intermediate principles between the ideals of Christian ethics that are universal and timeless and specific policy choices that have to relate to the laws, customs, and needs of different communities. [24] A "middle axiom" that directs attention to the needs of factory workers and their families might serve to draw the connection between the Christian love that sacrifices self for others and the legal rights that allow owners to retain profits without regard to the needs of their employees. In Britain, at the same time Niebuhr was writing reflections on proletarian and privileged social attitudes, Archbishop William Temple was developing a contemporary approach to economic justice that drew on the Catholic and Anglican traditions of natural law. Emil Brunner, a Swiss theologian, wrote about family, government, work, and religion as "orders of creation," the enduring institutions in society that give concrete form to God's will for human life. [25]

Niebuhr participated in these discussions, especially the work of the Oxford Conference, and he kept up a steady stream of editorials, lectures, and even campaign stump speeches that clearly proclaimed a Christian understanding of what equal justice requires, but he never explained in detail how to draw those connections. The important point for him was to keep Christian ideals at a critical distance from all concrete moral choices, including his own. The tradition of the Hebrew prophets, which comes to completion in Jesus' ethics, insists that God's goodness transcends the world's chaos and injustice. So the appropriate response to God is not to identify God's work with our own idea of justice. Maintaining that transcendence was for Niebuhr more important than having a method for arriving at moral decisions.

This clear identification of Christian realism with the tradition of Israel's prophets was, however, an important step beyond the theology of liberal Protestantism. Liberal theology had assumed that Christian faith was identical with the best insights of modern science and philosophy. Niebuhr now identified Christian realism with a tradition that stands at a critical distance from all other ways of understanding the human predicament. Instead of a history that is a progressive unfolding of Christian truth, we live in a world where "man has always been his own most vexing problem." [26] The world has never been able to accept the Christian answer to that problem, and history makes no steady progress toward it. Even Christians grasp the truth only when they are not too sure of their own virtue. [27]

Questions for Reflection

1. How did the history of the twentieth century differ from what theologians of the Social Gospel expected at its beginning? Are there aspects of the Social Gospel that remain important, despite the disappointment of these early hopes?

2. What is the role of conflict in the search for justice? Is Niebuhr right that justice requires that some people contend against us? Or is there an objective standard of justice that everyone can share?

3. How does Niebuhr understand Jesus' commandment to love God and our neighbor? How does he see this "impossible ideal" connected to the prophetic tradition? How is the love commandment misunderstood both by Christian liberalism and by Christian orthodoxy?

CHAPTER TWO

HUMAN NATURE

Prophetic faith avoids both sentimentality and despair. It keeps us from the cheerful assumption that our good deeds are steadily transforming the world into a better place and from the paralyzing fear that nothing we can do will make any difference. Prophetic faith replaces optimism with gratitude and despair with contrition, so that our choices and actions can be realistic and life remains meaningful, in spite of our finitude and limitations.

Such a faith contrasts sharply with other views that closely connect Christian faith and human progress or identify prophetic judgment with particular methods of social criticism. Niebuhr's new emphasis on biblical ideas, especially the tradition of the Hebrew prophets, continued his criticism of liberal Protestantism's high estimate of human possibilities, but it also marked a break with his own heavy reliance on Marxist social and economic ideas to explain the structural problems of modern industrial societies. This was not because he thought Marx was wrong. Marx understood the contradictions of modern economic life well, but Marxist criticism alone could not provide the foundation for a Christian understanding of society and its possibilities. What is needed is an "independent Christian ethic" that could survive both the disappointment of liberal hopes and the crises of modern social and economic organization that Marx more realistically analyzed. [1]

At this point, Niebuhr moved as close as he ever did to the reliance on the Word of God that characterized Karl Barth's ethics. For Barth, the Christian life depends solely on hearing that Word as it speaks to us through the biblical text, rejecting all fixed ideas about human nature or human possibilities that might provide a point of contact between concrete, specific divine judgment and general social theories or political programs. For Barth, theological ethics "should not make appeal to the truths supposed to lie in nature as creation of God, nor appeal to this, that, or other text in the Bible. Such ethics has to serve the Word of God, even as theology should. It must not anticipate that Word, nor may it obstruct that Word by setting up a human law." [2] Niebuhr's "independent Christian ethic" shares this separation from all human laws and programs, and even from all human interpretations of the biblical text. It is this apparent insistence on the uniqueness of prophetic faith that leads some interpreters to classify Niebuhr's theology as "neo-orthodox," despite his many disagreements with Barth and the other European theologians who share that identification.

Like Barth, Niebuhr questions claims about human nature that seem to put us in possession of absolute moral standards or promise control over the uncertainties of history. In the end, however, Niebuhr's project is different, and perhaps even bolder than Barth's radical refusal to allow any connection between human understanding and the Word of God. His independent Christian ethic is not radically separate from all other ways of thinking about God and the world, but critically engaged with each of them. Christians do not fool themselves into thinking that because they rely on the Word of God, they have no ideas about human nature, draw no conclusions from history, and follow no moral rules. The important thing is to identify the points of difference that distinguish the biblical understanding in specific ways from each of the alternatives. Theologians can integrate faith and science, as Protestant liberals attempted to do after Darwin revolutionized thinking about human origins. They can interpret human conflicts in social and economic terms, as Niebuhr did in *Moral Man and Immoral Society*. But the biblical understanding is never simply identical with these other interpretations, and prophetic faith always stands in judgment on their claims to have the last word about truth and justice. By being specific about how the biblical understanding of persons and society differs from the other theories they might employ, theologians can be more confident that they are using the tools of science, history, and social thought realistically, with an understanding of their limitations as well as their promise. Moreover, precisely because human intellect can never grasp the Word of God whole and in itself, this criticism of other systems and theories from a biblical viewpoint actually increases our understanding of the independent Christian ethic. Obedience to the Word of God is not, for Niebuhr, shutting out the other voices, but listening to them critically and in their own terms, in order that their real possibilities and limitations may become apparent. Nor should the scope of this comparison be confined to contemporary social and economic theories or to progressive views of history embraced by Social Gospel theologians in the recent past. All of Western thought, including religious and philosophical alternatives to Christianity in the ancient world and modern secular understandings from Renaissance humanism to Marxist materialism must be taken into consideration. [3] Only when we understand concretely how the biblical viewpoint differs from these alternatives can we claim to know the Word of God in the way it can be known by human minds.

This survey of the failed alternatives to Christian understanding is the ambitious project that Niebuhr undertakes in *The Nature and Destiny of Man*. An invitation to deliver the Gifford Lectures at the University of Edinburgh in 1939 inspired this longest and most systematic of his works. The Gifford Lectures are endowed by an 1885 bequest that stipulates the lecturers are to discuss natural theology "without reference to or reliance upon any supposed special exceptional or so-called miraculous revelation." [4] Instead of opening with a discussion of the obvious problems this directive poses for a Christian theologian, Niebuhr plunges directly into the task, comparing classical, Christian, and modern views of human nature, without any attempt to give the Christian view the special status of revealed truth, but with considerable confidence that he can demonstrate that the Christian view offers a more adequate assessment of both human possibilities and human evil than the alternatives. [5]

The gratitude and contrition that meaningful human life requires are thus not understood solely by reading Scripture nor learned exclusively within the Christian community. The need for both gratitude and contrition is grasped by comparison with ways of thinking and living that render one or the other unnecessary or impossible.

What distinguishes the biblical understanding of human nature is the tension it maintains between two contrasting themes, both of which are drawn from the first pages of the Hebrew Scriptures. First, human beings are created in the image of God (Genesis 1:26-27). We see in ourselves and others something that resembles God's freedom from determining necessities and God's transcendence of all boundaries. Reason, memory, and imagination ensure that we are never simply confined to given appearances, present time, and existing circumstances. We can understand why things are the way they are, and we can envision how they might be different. This freedom, however, is not identical with God's freedom. It is the freedom of a creature, set in a specific place in the whole creation that God has made. When we refuse that freedom and demand a larger one for ourselves, seeking not the image but the reality of God's power, we cut ourselves off from God and take up a struggle for survival that sets us at odds with one another and with the natural order (Genesis 3). "The high estimate of human stature implied in the concept of 'image of God' stands in paradoxical juxtaposition to the low estimate of human virtue in Christian thought. Man is a sinner. His sin is defined as rebellion against God." [6]

All of the possibilities for human life, including possibilities for the moral life, must be sought within this twofold, paradoxical human nature that is both the image of God and a sinful creature in rebellion against God. In this sense, Niebuhr follows the long tradition in Christian theology that derives ethics from human nature. His insistence that the study of human society and history validates the biblical understanding in ways that anyone should be able to grasp shares a great deal with the medieval theology of Thomas Aquinas, who bases morality on a natural law implanted in humanity by God and knowable by everyone through observing the order of things around them. Despite frequent objections to the specifics of Catholic teaching about the natural law, Niebuhr shares more with that tradition than with the theology of Barth, who bases ethics solely on the commandment of God known through Scripture, or with the Enlightenment philosopher Immanuel Kant, who argued that the basic formulations of the moral law are logically necessary. Moral judgments are made with the confidence appropriate to fallible human beings who have reflected carefully together on what their human nature requires, rather than with the assurance of faith or the certainty of logic.

Still, we should not place too much confidence in these shared moral judgments, nor should we be surprised when people disagree about what human nature requires. The central feature of *human* nature is the freedom that is part of the image of God. As creatures with reason, memory, and imagination, people cannot be described by a recitation of natural facts in the way that physical nature or biological life can be known. People are aware of themselves and their circumstances. They transcend the facts in a way that mirrors God's transcendence of creation. Consciousness introduces endless possibilities into our responses to the facts they are given, allowing human beings an "indefinite transcendence" over the circumstances in which they are born and the categories into which other people try to put them. [7] As a result, when someone tells us that nature requires a certain kind of sex or a certain kind of state, they are almost always wrong. Freedom is not so easily reduced to a set of rules. That is part of what it means to bear the image of God.

At the same time, these bearers of the divine image who are free to transcend their circumstances are nonetheless creatures. Their freedom is not absolute. It begins someplace. It is tied to the conditions of biological life, even if it is not determined by them. Freedom is limited by the mistakes people make and the willful blindness with which they sometimes refuse to face stubborn facts. It is subject to the vicissitudes of what other people do to us, and at some point, it ends in death.

Many of the other ways Western history has given us to think about human nature cannot grasp this tension between freedom and finitude that is central to the biblical understanding. For the ancient world, finitude itself was often the problem. The key to a good life—and often, too, the secret of immortality—was to escape the limitations of the body through ascetic discipline or mystical insight. True knowledge was thought to lie beyond the limitations of the senses. Plato's famous myth of the cave argues that what we think of as real because we know it through our senses is nothing but a shadow of true reality, which must be known by the mind alone. [8] Modern thinking, by contrast, often dismisses the freedom of the mind as the illusion. We must understand our lives as the product of social circumstances and biological realities, if we want to know who we are. Marx, Darwin, and Freud suggest that the only freedom we have comes from accepting and understanding the conditions of our finitude. Each argues in his own way that the idea that we are created in the image of God is a way of evading a difficult truth.

In setting out the Christian view of human nature, Niebuhr carefully distinguishes it from both of these ancient and modern alternatives. The difference begins with God as Creator and the consequences of that idea for our understanding of human finitude and freedom. "The Christian faith in God as Creator of the world transcends the canons and antinomies of rationality, particularly the antinomy between mind and matter, between consciousness and extension. God ... creates the world. This world is not God; but it is not evil because it is not God. Being God's creation, it is good." [9]

Thus, the finitude that limits our knowledge and ties us to a fragile, physical body is not itself an evil to be overcome. Our ties to a particular place and time and our birth into particular circumstances, with our own unique gifts and vulnerabilities, are to be received with the gratitude by which prophetic faith witnesses to the goodness of God's creation.

Gratitude, however, is a fragile emotion, and it usually does not last very long. The very freedom in which we become aware of our circumstances enables us to envision alternatives that we think we might prefer. I am grateful for my life, but I would be so much more grateful, it seems, if I were somewhat more rich, if I were more healthy, if life were not so short, if so much of it were not already spent.

Nor are such thoughts sheer ingratitude. A prudent awareness of our limitations is essential to wise living. Resistance to arbitrary constraints that others impose on us is essential to a sense of justice. Gratitude is not an uncritical acceptance of whatever circumstances in which we find ourselves. It is trust in the ultimate goodness of life and therefore in the meaningfulness of our existence in the present, despite its suffering, conflicts, and contradictions. This trust is the fruit of prophetic faith, and it is only partly supported by an analysis of the immediately available evidence.

Finitude by itself, then, does not threaten the goodness of life, but it does not prove it, either. Awareness of our circumstances elicits anxiety, as well as gratitude. To be conscious at all is to know that things might be different from what they are. Anxiety is born of the knowledge that things might be worse. Without the trust that comes from prophetic faith, we focus on our vulnerabilities and weaknesses. My health may fail. My job might disappear. I might not have the ability to complete the project I have proposed or to write this book that I have begun. At that point, other people begin to appear as threats or competitors, rather than companions, and prudence shades over into wary defensiveness or outright fear of everything that is different, other.

Anxiety, like the self-transcendence on which it depends, has no obvious limit. Langdon Gilkey summarizes the results vividly:

> Since our self-transcendence and the imagination that springs from it are unlimited, there are no possible limits to our anxiety about our security in either space or time. If we control our own valley, we can picture a new enemy on each

neighboring hill—and every succeeding hill. If we have sufficient food for the present winter, we can imagine now our hunger in the next year—and every subsequent year. [10]

So finitude is not evil, but finitude leads to anxiety. Nor is anxiety evil in itself, but it is "the internal description of the state of temptation," as Niebuhr puts it. [11] The evil that human beings can do, moral evil, originates in our responses to anxiety. The most important of these responses is that we seek to overcome our vulnerability through the use of our own power. We take control of circumstances that limit us and of other people who threaten us. If we are successful in this, we construct elaborate rationalizations to reassure ourselves that our success is deserved and that our control is permanent. Our talent entitles us to hold the job, and our charm and networking skills ensure that the fountain of prosperity will not run dry for us. Our virtue entitles us to victory, and more than that, the direction of history proves that we will shortly receive what we are entitled to. Those who oppose us, by contrast, deserve to fail, and we will by our own power see to it that they receive what they deserve. "Our anxiety—and hence our will to power and our greed and hence again our imperialism against every potential neighbor—is unlimited. Once we have become the center of our own world, conflict with and injustice toward every other inevitably arises." [12]

This movement in which anxiety generates both the structures of power and the beliefs that justify them is basic to human nature, and it may be seen in human life on every scale, from intimate personal relationships to the conflicts of imperial powers on the stage of history. [13] The dynamic is not only human and historical, however. In *Nature and Destiny*, Niebuhr is primarily concerned with the theological question of how this anxiety that is so deeply rooted in human nature figures in our relationship to God. For that reason, he names the result of anxiety "pride," and identifies it with the human self-glorification that is central to the biblical understanding of sin. [14] Pride is not only the raw exercise of power in an attempt to control other people. It is also the attempt to put the self in the place of God. The attempt, of course, requires that we deceive others about the purity of our motives and the legitimacy of our power, and finally it requires that we partly deceive ourselves. But because the self-deception is always incomplete, pride's self-centered answer to anxiety ends up by adding a new anxiety that the deception will fail and the self-justifying system will collapse under the weight of reality. "Thus," Niebuhr says, "sin compounds the insecurity of nature with a fresh insecurity of spirit." [15] Pride renders the gratitude of prophetic faith impossible, replacing it with an increasingly demanding self-reliance that is incapable of finding satisfaction in reality, precisely because it would have to be God in order to succeed.

Pride is for Niebuhr the most important form of sin, but it is not the only form. Niebuhr does not go in for highly nuanced, differentiated classifications of sins like the old Roman Catholic manuals of moral theology, designed to guide priests hearing confessions. He does not even recapitulate the list of seven "deadly" sins [16] that goes back to the early Church, but he does add alongside pride in its many different guises the forms of the sin he calls "sensuality." [17] This is easily misunderstood, as though Niebuhr were talking only about sexual sins. The acts and attitudes he has in mind are far broader, however, encompassing a whole range of ways in which people lose themselves in activities and relationships that are larger than themselves, so that their freedom is completely absorbed by the demands and possibilities offered by some limited good that becomes the object of their complete devotion. Romantic relationships can serve that purpose, but so, too, can maternal devotion to home and family, obsessive interest in a scholarly project, or total commitment to the goals marked out on a career path. What these diverse forms of sensuality have in common is that they make hard choices between goods unnecessary, because one good takes the place of all of them, and they render faith and hope irrelevant, because the object of desire is something immediately present.

In this way, sensuality is a kind of mirror image of pride. It deals with anxiety not by seizing control, but by surrendering itself so completely to whatever good is available that it has nothing to lose. Sensuality seems far less important than pride in shaping the political conflicts and historical transformations with which Niebuhr is most concerned, though it is arguable that the pride of tyrants and demagogues could not succeed without the sensuality of followers who give themselves totally to their movements. While Niebuhr suggests that sensuality is derived from pride, it could perhaps equally well be argued that the egotism central to pride is a sort of sensual devotion to the self. In any case, Niebuhr's critics have often suggested that his heavy emphasis on pride distorts the ways in which sensuality is equally basic to human nature.

It is possible to argue about the details of Niebuhr's account of pride and sensuality in human experience, but he seems to have succeeded in his main effort. He has relocated the central problem of human nature in our responses to the anxiety that invariably arises when human consciousness becomes aware of its own limitations. This problem, which can be described in experiential terms that are familiar to nearly everyone living with the uncertainties of the modern world, becomes comprehensible when we see human nature in biblical terms, based on a freedom that is a limited, but real, image of God's freedom. Neither the classical view that sees finitude as a problem to be overcome nor the modern naturalism that reduces human life to a product of natural and historical processes provides such a complete and realistic account of our experience. Indeed, Niebuhr's interpretation of sin as a response to the anxiety of finitude recasts the classical view as a version of the prideful denial of finitude, while modern scientific accounts of history and nature seem often to accept the sensual solution of reducing human life to systems and processes that are immediately available to the senses.

To complete this account of human nature, Niebuhr must do two things more. First, the initial identification of pride and sensuality as the key forms of sin in experience must be integrated into a more complete theological account of sin that is consistent with historic Christian understandings. Second, Niebuhr must return to the basic purpose of all of his theological explorations, beginning with *An Interpretation of Christian Ethics*. He must show how this account of human nature makes a meaningful moral life possible. That has never been an easy task for Christian theologians who take sin seriously, but it is important for the political and historical judgments that responsible Christians must make.

Niebuhr's account of how anxiety leads to sin suggests, perhaps, that we might break the whole cycle of insecurity, pride, and unjust power by reacting differently to the experience of anxiety at the outset. Suppose that instead of trying to master insecurity with our own power, we chose to trust the goodness of creation. Why must anxiety always lead to sin? Isn't gratitude equally possible in human nature?

Niebuhr's answer is that trust is always present as an ideal possibility, but to suggest that we have a simple choice between pride and gratitude ignores realities in experience and basic points of Christian teaching. We do not confront the ideal possibility as ideal persons, choosing before we have any experience of anxiety or pride. We come to see the possibility of trust, if we see it at all, only after we are already caught in the cycle of pride, power, and deception. We can understand how trust and gratitude would work, so it would be a mistake to say that we *necessarily* respond to anxiety with pride or sensuality, as though those were the only possibilities that human nature allows. But we never ask the question without realizing that we are already acting unjustly toward our neighbors, already deceiving ourselves and others in the way that sin requires. Sin is not necessary to human nature, but it is inevitable in human experience. The Christian view "affirms that the evil in man is a consequence of his inevitable though not necessary unwillingness to acknowledge his dependence, to accept his finiteness and to admit his insecurity, an unwillingness which involves him in the vicious circle of accentuating the insecurity from which he seeks escape." [18]

In this idea that sin is inevitable but not necessary, Niebuhr provides an experiential account of the Christian doctrine of "original sin," the idea that all human beings not only bear guilt for their own individual sins, but also share in the first act of disobedience by which Adam and Eve turned away from the innocence in which God had created them and acquired knowledge of good and evil. Original sin makes it clear that we cannot save ourselves from sin simply by resolving to make different choices in the future. We require God's assistance to overcome the inevitable choices by which we have already tried to put ourselves in God's place when we begin to understand our own problem.

To say that sin is deeply embedded in our society and in our own thinking, even before we become aware of it, resonated with the generation that had survived the First World War only to see the world turn to totalitarian dictators and plunge itself into global conflict for a second time. The slide toward war in the decade before Niebuhr delivered his Gifford lectures even reinforced the sense that sin is inevitable in human nature. Still, the terminology caused Niebuhr some difficulty with his readers, and in a new preface written in 1963, he expressed some regret that a literal reading of these traditional symbols might have obscured his meaning.

Niebuhr regarded the story of Adam, Eve, and the serpent in Genesis 3 as a "myth" or a "symbol," by which he meant a narrative or an image that conveys a truth that cannot be fully expressed in purely rational terms. [19] Myth and symbol are required whenever we speak of God, and if we give an account of human nature in theological terms, it will contain elements like the tension between freedom and dependence, which cannot be fully articulated in a linear, consistent way. The symbol of the sinful creature who is also created in the image of God conveys the point more adequately than the systematic elaborations of it in our theology. The fall and original sin likewise convey the truth that sin is "inevitable, but not necessary," even if that way of putting the point seems like a contradiction in purely rational terms.

Steeped in biblical language since childhood and accustomed to thinking in theological terms, Niebuhr readily turned to Christian language to explicate the structures of human nature and explain the tensions in ordinary human experience. He was somewhat surprised when secular readers, and even some of his liberal Protestant contemporaries, were distracted by literalistic interpretations that treated the symbol of the fall as an event that occurred in history or engaged in speculations about the mechanism by which original sin is transmitted from generation to generation. Two decades later, Niebuhr understood better how the traditional language could be a barrier to understanding, but he did not discount the truth behind the symbol. Neither did he conclude that the language of theology is a closed system of meanings that can only interpret experience for those who share it in its entirety. Niebuhr differs both from his liberal Protestant predecessors who were prepared to discard biblical images and doctrinal concepts that conflict with modern science and from his postmodern theological critics who insist that Christian doctrine is a system of meaning that is necessarily incomprehensible to those who do not share the faith. *Nature and Destiny* indicates in some detail the understanding of doctrinal truth and biblical interpretation in his work as a whole. The language and symbols of Christian faith are not self-explanatory, but they can be related to human experience in every era, and when those connections are drawn well, the Christian understanding will make better sense of history and human experience than any of the alternative explanations.

It must be said, however, that connecting doctrine and experience is not easy, and the misunderstandings are not only modern ones. Remember that what Niebuhr is trying above all to do is to give an account of human nature that will sustain a meaningful moral life despite the evils that work against it, in the world and in ourselves. The doctrine of original sin provided Niebuhr with an understanding that injustice and violence cannot simply be reversed by good people deciding to make different choices. The Social Gospel preacher's vision of a society transformed by Christians asking "What would Jesus do?" cannot be supported by experience or by Christian doctrine. But understanding the pervasiveness of sin has not always motivated people to act against it. If sin is part of our human nature, perhaps it is futile to resist it. It may even seem that the responsibility for this overwhelming pride and sensuality lies elsewhere—with Adam and Eve, in a too-literal misreading of the story of the fall, or with God who created us with this anxiety-provoking freedom.

Niebuhr's insistence that sin is "inevitable, but not necessary" is part of his effort to address this problem. In a lengthy chapter on original sin and human responsibility, he joins a line of realistic thinkers stretching back at least to Augustine who have sought to demonstrate that people are still accountable for the particular choices that take them into the cycle of insecurity and injustice, even though there is no real possibility of avoiding it. [20] Original sin does not destroy human freedom or end human responsibility, despite the persistent misunderstanding of those who throughout Christian history have seen it as a reason for enduring evil passively while waiting for God's redemption. To say that sin is the inevitable, but not necessary, outcome of human freedom summarizes a complex understanding of the moral life that is consistent with both historic Christian doctrine and contemporary experience.

Niebuhr's Christian realism, however, needs something more than an abstract accountability for the choices that have been shaped by anxiety, pride, and prior sin. Responsibility as he understands it involves a willingness to make discriminating choices between greater and lesser evils, and this, too, seems to be threatened by an understanding that sin is a pervasive feature of every human life and every system of ideas that people create to organize their power and explain their injustices. Niebuhr had confronted this problem in his debate with his brother over the Christian responses to Japanese aggression in the early 1930s. [21] As he wrote the lectures on sin and human responsibility for *Nature and Destiny*, Niebuhr contemplated a world in which the Western democracies were bracing for war against Hitler's Germany. Pride and self-righteous power seemed increasingly salient for an understanding of international relations, but was it really possible that Christian faith had nothing to say except that all parties to the conflict were equally sinful?

Niebuhr's answer was to pair the inevitable, but not necessary, human sin with another equally paradoxical formulation of human responsibility: equality of sin and inequality of guilt. [22] All systems of government and social organization compound natural insecurity with a contrived insecurity of spirit to justify the power that those who hold it are afraid to surrender. No nation can claim that it is purely good and its enemies are purely evil, or that its system promises perfect freedom while its rivals would condemn the world to perpetual slavery. A choice between democracy and totalitarianism framed in those terms will fail, because its terms are unrealistic. But that does not mean that the audience gathered in Edinburgh for the Gifford lectures had no moral reason to choose parliamentary democracy instead of a Nazi *Führer* or that they could not explain their choice in terms that would make sense to the rest of the world. Guilt is an assessment of the consequences of the pursuit of power and security. If both totalitarian and democratic systems share equally in the deceptions and self-justifications that sin creates, it is nonetheless possible to measure the costs of the totalitarian search for security—the repression of dissent, the aggression against neighboring countries, the sacrifice of family, religious, and cultural values for the advancement of the nation—and conclude that those who care about justice must choose democracy and reject totalitarianism, even though both systems fall short of perfect justice. An adequate understanding of sin even assists this discriminating judgment, because it gives us a critical eye for the deceptions and self-justifications by which the guilty obscure their guilt before the world. Finally, although Niebuhr had no doubt where the greater guilt lay in the conflict the world was facing at the end of the 1930s, he insisted that an adequate understanding of sin is also essential for the recognition of our own guilt.

While the idea that sin is inevitable but not necessary nicely captures the understanding of human freedom and responsibility that is central to the Christian doctrine of original sin, the paradox of equal sin and unequal guilt is not quite so satisfactory as the basis for responsible choices. Niebuhr's formulation in *Nature and Destiny* suggests that guilt is an objective measure of the consequences of actions:

> Guilt is distinguished from sin in that it represents the objective and historical consequences of sin, for which the sinner must be held responsible. It is the guilt of the sinner that his self-love results in the consequence of broken or unhappy homes, of children made unhappy by their parents, of peoples destroyed by wars which were prompted by the vanity of their rulers, of the poverty of the victims of greed and the unhappiness of the victims of jealousy and envy. [23]

This emphasis on the objective consequences of sin is intended to preserve the distinction between aggressors and their victims, but if all are indeed sinners, this quantitative emphasis on consequences may blur the distinction it seeks to maintain. It seems to put a premium on limiting the damages and to make little provision for the losses that must sometimes be sustained to preserve important values. Short months after Niebuhr delivered the Gifford Lectures, the British government would consider whether to sustain the war alone should France fall to the Germans. [24] Given the forces arrayed against Britain and the inevitable costs of continued fighting, would surrender be the best of the bad options? If guilt is measured by the consequences of our actions, would surrender have been the less guilty choice?

A full account of how responsible choice is possible under the conditions of sin would require further development of Niebuhr's thought, including more specific consideration of what can be said about democracy in relation to totalitarianism beyond the fact that both are involved in sinful exercises of power and self-justification. What he had provided in the first part of *Nature and Destiny*, however, was what seemed most essential at the moment—an account of human nature that allowed for both gratitude and contrition in response to a realistic understanding of sin and evil. The evil on the historical horizon made the reassertion of prophetic faith the central theological task of the time.

Questions for Reflection

1. What are the strengths and weaknesses of Niebuhr's method of comparing the Christian understanding of human nature to various historical alternatives? Are there distinctive elements of the Christian proclamation that tend to be lost when it is compared to other philosophical and religious claims? Or do we need the contrasts to help us understand what the Christian understanding really is?

2. How does Niebuhr understand the idea that human beings are created in the image of God? What are the characteristics of human beings in which this image is most clearly seen?

3. How does Niebuhr understand the Christian doctrine of original sin? If the anxiety that leads to sin is always part of human nature, how can sin itself be an individual responsibility? Could anxiety be overcome? How does the figure of Jesus as portrayed in the Gospels help Niebuhr to answer that question?

CHAPTER THREE

HUMAN DESTINY

In his major works, Niebuhr's purpose is always to give Christians a way of thinking that will enable responsible moral choices. Above all, that means being realistic about the possibilities and limitations of all action, so that our efforts are not wasted on sentimental gestures that fail to touch the real problems, or self-righteous demands that ignore our own involvement in the problems we are trying to solve. But this political realism must be accompanied by an understanding that locates human action in a meaningful moral universe, or we may yield to cynicism and despair. Thinking that nothing we can do makes any difference is as dangerous to responsible choices as the naïve belief that we can transform the world just by asking what Jesus would do.

Realistic knowledge of human nature is an important part of what we need to make responsible choices. We have to understand that power shapes relationships between groups and nations, and people do not give up power willingly. We need a critical eye for the explanations by which people justify the power they have, and we need to be self-critical about our own claims to knowledge and virtue. We must learn to recognize the characteristic forms of pride and sensuality by which individuals and groups deal with their anxieties, and we need a broad education about the forces that shape contemporary society as well as the classical and modern theories that are in continual tension with the biblical viewpoint, with its paradoxes of freedom and finitude.

Because of the freedom that is at its heart, our knowledge of human nature can never be static, orderly, and complete. The variations we observe in history and in different human societies are as important as the regularities of nature, although theological ideas about "nature" or the "orders of creation" tend to forget this.

Nevertheless, a great deal can be known about human nature, and that knowledge is a reliable guide to responsible choice and action. On this fundamental point, Niebuhr is closer to Thomas Aquinas and the tradition of natural law that goes back to the Stoics and early Christian philosophers than he is to Karl Barth's theology of obedience or to existential philosophies that deny that humans have any nature except the one they create for themselves. Without the knowledge of human nature summarized in the first part of *Nature and Destiny*, responsible action would be impossible. We do not need Niebuhr's lectures to acquire this knowledge, of course. Much of what we need to know about human nature is available in history and ordinary experience, particularly as these are understood through the prophetic tradition in scripture. Faith coordinates this knowledge into a "deeper and wider system of coherence," but faith does not contradict the rest of what we know. [1]

Still, knowledge of human nature is not all we need for meaningful moral action. We might avoid the easy choices of sentimentality and the excesses of pride and still see no reason to think beyond the limits of a prudent self-interest. Realistic understanding of the illusions that shape the actions of others around us may, in fact, tempt us to cynical manipulation of those who are not as clear-sighted as we are. It is hard to see what the gratitude and contrition of prophetic faith have to do with that kind of realism about human nature.

Christian faith, then, is more than an understanding of human nature. The difference between the Christian realist and the self-interested cynic also involves a different understanding of *human destiny*.

Things would be much simpler, of course, if we could view history with the confidence in human progress that was so widely shared by Americans at the end of the nineteenth century. Caring for the poor, wanting justice for our neighbors, and seeking peace in the world would then be a matter of joining the direction in which history is moving. There might be times when our short-term, selfish interests would dictate different choices. Even optimists sometimes have to make moral decisions. But over the long run, loving our neighbors is also the most successful course of action, and if enough people begin to understand that and act accordingly, the long run need not be very long. From this perspective, Jesus' teaching that we should love God and our neighbor is not only the Great Commandment. It is good advice, too. Jesus himself becomes the prime example of how we should live in order to be part of the human progress that God intends. [2]

By the end of the fourth decade of the twentieth century, the direction of history was far less clear. As Niebuhr delivered his second series of Gifford Lectures, history seemed perhaps to be on the side of Stalin's Communists, who were consolidating their authoritarian regime in the Soviet Union. Certainly, recent history had favored Hitler's Reich and the Empire of Japan, which were demonstrating their prosperity and military superiority by becoming the dominant powers in Europe and Asia. History was providing shockingly little evidence that Jesus' law of love was indeed the law of life. It might be, as Niebuhr argued in *An Interpretation of Christian Ethics*, that love is involved in all moral judgments and is the basis of "even the most minimal social standards," [3] but the connection between that morality and the course of history was becoming hard to see. Could people who understood the ambiguities of human nature as well as Niebuhr did have any reason to think that their moral judgments made any difference in that kind of history?

Niebuhr's answer to that question begins with the Christian affirmation that Jesus is the Christ anticipated by prophetic faith. Jesus is not simply a moral ideal whom we are called individually to emulate, in the way that the Social Gospel taught us to answer moral questions by asking what Jesus would do. Jesus is the expected Christ, the Chosen One who manifests God's power over history within history.

Just as the biblical view that humanity is both image of God and sinful creature differs from all the philosophical and religious alternatives for understanding of human nature, the expectation of a Christ creates a different understanding of human destiny. [4] The promise of God's presence within history suggests that meaningful human life is not to be sought in a changeless realm of ideas outside of history, nor is human meaning to be found in natural forces, so that the meaning of life lies in its absorption into a natural order known by scientific methods. Where a Christ is not expected, humanity has a nature, but not a destiny. Prophetic faith finds meaning within history, because history is where people encounter God and find direction for their lives and actions. That is what Niebuhr means by "destiny."

Christianity shares with the prophetic tradition this idea that destiny gives meaning to human life. To see the life and teaching of Jesus of Nazareth as the fulfillment of prophetic expectation, however, changes the meaning of history in important ways. The expected messiah appears not as the triumphant vindicator of his people's righteousness, but as the Suffering Servant whose teaching of God's love is rejected by his own people. Jesus does not triumph in confrontation with the powers of history. Roman authorities misunderstand his appearance as a part of a troublesome pattern of provincial unrest, and he is tortured and killed by them. His resurrection does not change these historical facts. The resurrection does not accomplish within history the transfer of power that Jesus' disciples wanted and that the Romans were trying to prevent. [5] The resurrection is rather a sign that God's fulfillment does not depend on human power, and God's completion of history will involve a judgment on those who believe that they have shaped it. The judgment that gives meaning to history is radically different from judgments about success and failure.

At the same time, Jesus' presence in history is not just a story of failure. If that were so, the meaning of life would still have to be sought outside of history. Jesus transforms the lives of those around him, and his law of love reveals a connection between people that is more basic than the defensive and self-seeking constructions by which they isolate themselves from one another. Jesus' defeat, like the human sin that brought it about, was "inevitable, but not necessary." [6] It is inevitable, because God does not finally defeat sin within history; but not nec-essary, because love is nonetheless the law of life. [7]

Perhaps because of the long influence of the prophetic tradition shaping Western culture, people today are likely to share the biblical view that mean-ingful life is to be sought within history. As Niebuhr observes, modern culture ostensibly rejects the biblical view entirely, but retains more than it realizes. [8] Modern people do not readily take the view of Platonic philosophers, supposing that the solutions to all their conflicts are to be found by contemplating truths that exist outside of history. If modern people doubt that history is meaningful, they are more likely to dissolve historic conflicts in the regularities of nature, so that wars are simply highly developed expressions of primate aggression, and our commitments are determined by our genes, rather than by what we believe and choose. Most modern people, however, find meaning in political choices between democracy and authoritarianism, in their religious community, or in loyalty to their country or to their ethnic group. They also find meaning in more personal choices about vocation, and about where to live, and how, and with whom. They see all of these as commitments, not as historical accidents or nat-ural necessities.

Modern people do not doubt that history is meaningful, but they find it more difficult to see that meaning in Jesus as the fulfillment of prophetic faith. Instead, they seek clues to the meaning of life in what is successful, or even in what is cur-rently popular. Life is meaningful because I enjoy the things that show up in the style sections of the daily newspaper, or because I have a job in cutting-edge technology, or because my political affiliation is with the majority party, or even because I attend a growing church where worship speaks to the ways that people feel about their faith now. Finding this sort of meaning in history, of course, requires a certain confidence that present trends will continue. Perhaps more seriously, it requires a confidence in my own loyalties and choices that eliminates ambiguity, so that my party, faith, or project is completely right, and others are completely wrong. People who ignore the ambiguities of history in this way may remind us of the dangerous fanatic whom Niebuhr portrays at the end of *Moral Man and Immoral Society*. Ambiguity is also rejected in the shifting enthusiasms of an affluent, consumer-oriented society where many identities and loyalties are on offer, and people take them up one after another, always confident that *this* one will deliver the meaningful life that it promises.

Both the iron-willed fanatic and the fickle consumer thus derive meaning from the expectation of success. A tragic viewpoint, by contrast, allows modern people to find meaning without requiring them to pick the winner in history's conflicts. Commitment to one's own ideal and truths can be sustained in spite of failure, especially if the failure is viewed as inevitable. One simply makes a com-mitment and holds to it without alteration, regardless of success and in spite of failure. When circumstances change and success ends, meaning comes from nobly enduring the inevitable loss.

This tragic view of life has much in common with the Christian understanding, as Niebuhr recognized. [9] Christianity, too, is prepared to endure suffering and recognizes that love will inevitably experience failure. There is, however, this important difference: Tragedy, like success, eliminates ambiguity. In tragedy, everything that is noble is destroyed, and everything that is destroyed is noble, including even the tragic flaw that leads to destruction. Tragedy is the end of meaningful history, in the sense that nothing survives by which good and evil might then be judged. The identification of the good with one's own choices and commitments is so complete that failure means the loss of the good itself.

In the end, both the pursuit of success and the acceptance of tragedy seek to derive a meaningful history from events in history. The various ways of pursuing success simply take life's meaning from what prevails in history's inevitable conflicts, believing that this success will continue unbroken to the end of history, or at least that a forgiving political and cultural environment will permit a timely transfer of loyalties to the next big thing. Acceptance of tragedy foregoes the hope or expectation of vindication at the end of history, thinking that this is a weakness that belongs to Christianity. The tragic understanding sustains meaning by a commitment so identified with its view of its own worth that failure of this self-understanding results in destruction of the self, but destruction of the self also marks the end of meaning. No final judgment in which the values around which life has organized itself are both judged and redeemed could compensate the tragic hero for the loss of this self-constructed nobility. [10]

The meaning of history fulfilled in Christ is different from either of these. Just as original sin should not be confused with an event at the beginning of history, the fulfillment of history in Christ cannot be confused with an event that vindicates the Christian view of life, either within history or at the end of it. Judgment is not a final tally of history's results that takes place at some point in time. Judgment reveals the reality of human nature, with its mixture of divine image and human sin, at every point within history. Judgment restores the ambiguities that both pursuit of success and acceptance of tragedy try to eliminate from life.

> The love of Christ thus always stands in a double relation to the strivings and achievements, the virtues and wisdoms of history. Insofar as they represent developments of the goodness of creation it is their fulfillment. Insofar as they represent false completions which embody the pride and the power of individuals and nations, of civilizations and cultures, it is their contradiction. [11]

Christ's fulfillment of history is thus something quite different from the literal image of the separation of the saved and the damned that we see, for example, in Michelangelo's paintings in the Sistine Chapel. The love of Christ reveals the difference between good and evil, but it also shows us how good and evil are all mixed up in history. The clarity of the final separation contrasts with the confusion and ambiguity evident as the law of love makes itself relevant at every point within history.

Christian writers have emphasized this difference between present facts and final judgment at least since Augustine. [12] That recognition of ambiguity is one reason Niebuhr thinks of Augustine as an early Christian realist. What the prospect of a final separation of good and evil beyond history teaches about life here and now is that there is evil in every good and good in every evil. This is a theological affirmation, not a report on his historical research. It is the meaning of a divine judgment that transcends history, but is relevant to every point within it.

This is a difficult lesson to accept. We would prefer to think that our belief in final judgment and the fulfillment of history authorizes us to make unambiguous distinctions between good and evil in our own situation. But having a destiny does not lift us that far above the limitations of our human nature. We cannot anticipate the final judgment of good and evil, because we are too much involved in both good and evil to see them clearly from God's perspective. As Oliver O'Donovan has recently suggested, the church's witness to God's judgment is that no human agency can claim to exercise judgment in this final sense. Of course, judgments of a more limited sort are essential to human life, and judgment is especially the work of government, which backs up those judgments with power and punishment. Government is therefore particularly tempted to confuse its judgments with the ultimate one. What Niebuhr observed in history was that governments almost always yield to that temptation. "The understanding that no political society can be entirely free of idolatry," O'Donovan writes, "was Reinhold Niebuhr's most enduring insight." [13]

The Christian realist, then, must chart a course between cynicism and idolatry in every moral decision. This is particularly important, and particularly difficult, in political choices, which make greater claims to shape the future and affect the lives of more people.

Without attention to God's judgment, expressed in the command to love our neighbors, our decisions quickly become self-interested. The idea that there is a final unity behind the conflicts in our immediate experience ceases to influence our choices. The moral life is reduced to a series of choices between competing interests in which the objective is to advance our own interests or those of our group as far as possible. Doing the right thing is reduced to doing what appears to make us stronger and to weaken our competitors and adversaries.

Of course, some measure of self-interest is unavoidable. No one who understands human nature as Niebuhr does could fail to see that. That is why Niebuhr insisted that the moral questions in politics are about justice, not love. Concern for equal justice is the closest approximation to love that human beings can manage in the large, complex groups that make up modern society. But even here, it is important to recognize the element of judgment. Every system of justice devised by courts and legislatures implicitly recognizes the possibility of a higher, more equal justice than the justice it has so far achieved. Without that awareness of limits and openness to judgment in our legal and political systems, justice becomes just another tool for advancing the interests of those in power.

> The Christian conception of the relation of historical justice to the love of the Kingdom of God is a dialectical one. Love is both the fulfillment and the negation of all achievements of justice in history. Or expressed from the opposite standpoint, the achievements of justice in history may rise in indeterminate degrees to find their fulfillment in a more perfect love and brotherhood; but each new level of fulfillment also contains elements which stand in contradiction to perfect love. There are therefore obligations to realize justice in indeterminate degrees; but none of the realizations can assure the serenity of perfect fulfillment. [14]

What Niebuhr argues in his account of human destiny, then, is that every search for justice that is more than a cynical attempt to use the language of justice for selfish purposes expresses a version of the judgment that the law of love makes on all of our achievements and choices. We seek justice, but we know that every system of justice we can create stands partly condemned by the very ideas of justice that went into its making. Short of God's ultimate judgment, there is no escape from this dialectic in which every achievement of justice demands a further effort. To suppose that we have arrived at justice is to fall into that idolatry from which no political society is free.

Because of this endless dialectic of judgment, Niebuhr realized that no political or economic system could claim to be such a clear expression of God's will that all Christians would be required to support it. This may have been a clear implication of his criticisms of both proletarian and privileged classes as early as *Moral Man and Immoral Society*, but the temptation to offer a theological endorsement of American democracy became much stronger when the nation was fully involved in the Second World War and in the Cold War struggle against Communism that followed. Niebuhr became an ardent anti-Communist, but this political commitment never distracted him from the main theological point. "We have come now to the fairly general conclusion that there is no 'Christian' economic or political system," he wrote in 1957. "But there is a Christian attitude toward all systems and schemes of justice." [15] The first element in that Christian attitude is the relentless pursuit of justice, irrespective of present levels of achievement and without regard to the justice or injustice of alternative systems.

Part of Niebuhr's genius as an essayist and social critic was his ability to sustain this critical perspective, even with respect to causes and commitments he strongly supported. He never sought to escape the critical question by arguing that we are more just than our competitors and rivals, or by pointing to how much more just our society is today than it was in the past. In the midst of the

Cold War, Niebuhr warned Americans of the risks of overstating the case for democracy "when the modicum of error in truth is not challenged and the modicum of truth in a falsehood is not rescued and cherished." After the achievements of the Civil Rights movement, he still worried about the fate of minorities in a "self-righteous" nation. [16]

The critical attitude is essential, but taken by itself, this emphasis on divine judgment does not make the necessary choices. Indeed, a prophetic grasp of the limits of our moral answers may lead to paralyzing uncertainty, smug complacency, or bleak despair. We have already noted Reinhold Niebuhr's exchange with his brother over whether "doing nothing" could be a faithful response to God's judgment on all sides in the Asian crisis of the early 1930s. We can imagine Christians having similar reactions to conflicts in the Middle East today, or perhaps to contentious political issues at home, like abortion or affirmative action. Sometimes it seems that all sides are too convinced of their own righteousness and too quick to equate compromise with surrender. Depending on our own circumstances and temperament, we may react to this impasse by wavering uncertainly between the choices, piously giving thanks that our faith puts the resolution of these issues in God's hands, or falling into despair over the futility of human conflict. In each of these responses, the commitment to ultimate justice gets in the way of immediate decisions.

That is why, for Niebuhr, the "critical attitude" that questions the justice of every course of action must be paired with a

> responsible attitude, which will not pretend to be God nor refuse to make a decision between political answers to a problem because each answer is discovered to contain a moral ambiguity in God's sight. We are men, not God; we are responsible for making choices between greater and lesser evils, even when our Christian faith, illuminating the human scene, makes it quite apparent that there is no pure good in history, and probably no pure evil, either. [17]

Responsible decisions are made between possibilities that are really available to us here and now. Election campaigns are about alternative plans for providing health care, or funding education, or reforming welfare. They are not about ideal standards of justice. Presidents and prime ministers usually make decisions about war and peace based on "conditions on the ground," the facts of the moment, and not on ideological commitments or grand strategies. On the whole, Reinhold Niebuhr thought this focus on the concrete, specific, present situation was a good thing. He was a master of this sort of analysis, and he gave the same energy and attention to political causes that he gave to theological and ethical principles. Today, when campaigns often turn to "values voters" who will decide political questions on the basis of religious commitments, we should perhaps remind ourselves of Niebuhr's idea that political choices should be responsible, as well as faithful. Before the presidential election in 1952, he wrote that "political decisions must be more circumspect than Christian decisions in America have been either on the right or on the left. Nothing is clearer than that ideologically consistent political positions have on the whole been refuted by history, while healthy nations have preserved freedom and extended justice by various pragmatic policies which borrowed from various strategies." [18] In politics, there are no ideal choices mapped out in the Bible or set before us by faith in advance. But there are many responsible choices, defined by expert knowledge and selected by a broad democracy that exercises its control over time and through a variety of leaders. We will follow this connection between democracy and responsibility more closely in the next two chapters.

The combination of critical attitude and responsible attitude that makes up the Christian attitude toward all political and economic systems might thus be described as confidence for the long run and choices for the here and now. Niebuhr's confidence in God's judgment and in his own analysis never translates into a belief that he can predict the outcome of our choices in enough detail to justify a decision on the basis of the expected consequences. He insists that every effort to establish justice raises the possibility of a more perfect justice than the one we have just established, but he does not see this as continuous progress. Sometimes, new forms of justice reintroduce old injustices that have been forgotten, so that we are no longer vigilant against them, and Niebuhr became increasingly concerned about the ironies of history in which complex circumstances and unanticipated changes gave us results exactly opposite to what we expected. Alertness to these ironies is particularly important in American politics, where the extent of our resources and our ability to impose our power, first on a vast continental territory and then on the wider world, often lead us to expect more control over future events than a knowledge of our history would justify. [19] Responsible choices recognize the limits of our knowledge and power, and they have to be reviewed at regular intervals to see how events are really developing. Responsible choices try to correct for the ironies of history, because they recognize that the irony cannot be overcome.

Both the critical attitude and the responsible attitude are essential to the moral life, as Niebuhr recognized already in his *Interpretation of Christian Ethics*. [20] What has become more clear by the end of *The Nature and Destiny of Man* is that this tension depends on a theological account of human destiny, as well as an acute analysis of human nature. Niebuhr's way of reading the Bible does not treat God's judgment as an event in history, not even as an event that comes at the very end of history. We cannot make sense of divine judgment either by seeing it as the predictable outcome of historical progress toward which all events and choices lead or by waiting for it as an eschatological reversal that will render all of our choices within history irrelevant. Judgment points to the mixture of good and evil in every choice and every experience. This does not mean that Niebuhr's idea of divine judgment confuses good and evil and reduces history to a relativistic muddle. The difference between good and evil is clear enough. But it is equally clear that persons, institutions, and political systems do not represent good and evil in pure form. "The final enigma of history is therefore not how the righteous will gain victory over the unrighteous, but how the evil in every good and the unrighteousness of the righteous is to be overcome." [21] That is the tension that gives meaning to our moral choices. Without it, we settle into a resigned or complacent waiting for God to work it all out on God's own terms, or we yield to the fury of the fanatic who cannot bear the ambiguity of real experience and is determined to impose the order that God, or history, or nature requires.

Those who believe that judgment enters history in the Christ are not surprised that history's verdict turns out always to be ambiguous, so they do not expect that their search for justice will ever yield perfect justice. But they also know that history's verdict is not final, so they do not let the ambiguity of history tempt them into a cynical pursuit of self-interest. They remain critical and responsible.

The question that remains is whether we can know this truth about human destiny in the same way that we know truths about human nature, drawing our confidence from experience and sharing our evidence with those who do not share our faith. The short answer to that question is no. Without the idea of a meaning that transcends the evidence of history, judgment is impossible, and our moral lives are limited to the calculation of the best consequences for the most people. [22] Niebuhr writes, "No Christ could validate himself as the disclosure of a hidden divine sovereignty over history or as a vindication of the meaningfulness of history, if a Christ were not expected." [23] With respect to our knowledge of human destiny, Niebuhr can be as insistent as Barth that the Word must create its own hearing. To understand why history is meaningful in the way that Niebuhr sets it out, we must first share the prophetic tradition's expectation of a Christ, and we must encounter the Christ of the Christian Scriptures, whose good news elicits both love and rejection, and whose sovereignty is apparent in history only to those who share the expectation and the encounter.

Nevertheless, Niebuhr believed that a "limited rational validation of the truth of the Gospel is possible." [24] This limited rational validation looks less like a logical argument or a scientific proof than like ordinary, practical political wisdom. Like political wisdom, realistic Christianity does not expect events to provide proofs or permanent solutions. It knows that the arguments will continue indefinitely. Like practical politics, realistic Christianity can accept defeat without losing hope and without losing its critical perspective on events. This connection between a certain kind of Christianity that Niebuhr would term "realistic" and a kind of politics that we would label "democracy" became more and more important in Niebuhr's work after he completed his masterful survey of human nature and human destiny.

Questions for Reflection

1. How does Niebuhr think that the expectation of a Christ changes our understanding of history? What is distinctive about the Christian claim that Jesus of Nazareth is the appearance of that expected Christ within history?

2. How is a critical attitude toward all system schemes of justice related to a responsible attitude in Niebuhr's thought? Is it possible to make a moral commitment to choices that fall short of the requirements of justice when subjected to a critical examination?

3. To what extent is it possible to provide a rational validation of the Christian view of history? What evidence could a Christian provide to a skeptical observer that history is meaningful in the way that Christian faith says that it is?

CHAPTER FOUR

DEMOCRACY

Christian realism" was the name that Reinhold Niebuhr and his colleagues gave to their way of thinking about theology and ethics. They began by trying to be more realistic than most Americans had recently been about the prospects for justice and social change. Progress is not assured, the Christian realists warned. Indeed, it is often reversed by the ironies of history. Resistance to change will be greater than we expect, and the complexities of economic life and modern politics make it difficult to organize effectively across differences of race, wealth, and power.

Beyond realism about change and resistance, Niebuhr especially warned that we have to be realistic about ourselves. The reason change is difficult is that we ourselves are part of the problem. We have an interest in things the way they are, and therefore we do not want change as much as we think we do.

Part of what Niebuhr's Christian realism provided was a theological understanding of these stubborn facts. Self-interest and self-deception are rooted in original sin. They are part of our human nature in ways that cannot easily be overcome. From the beginning, we do not trust God in the way we would have to do if we were to work for justice without fear and without trying to protect our own interests.

In light of these realities, finally, we need to be realistic about strategies for change. Appeals to love will not work, and even justice is a rather remote ideal for people trying to organize a labor union, fight for decent housing, or secure the right to vote. In international affairs, despite the enthusiasm for Christian pacifism after the First World War, Christian realists argued that nations have to be prepared to use force to defend themselves and protect weaker nations from aggression. Even within the nation, *Moral Man and Immoral Society* suggested, we cannot expect to change the alignments of racial discrimination or economic power without the application of some force, even if that is nonviolent force.

What Christian realists recognize and idealists forget is that "justice will require that some men shall contend against them." [1]

This was an important message to Christian pacifists still recoiling from the horrors of trench warfare or sentimental followers of the Social Gospel who still hoped to change the world by asking what would Jesus do, but by the time Niebuhr had completed his Gifford Lectures, and the second volume of *The Nature and Destiny of Man* appeared in 1943, America was deeply involved in the Second World War. Finding people willing to contend against us did not seem to be a problem. The question in many minds was whether Christian realists, with their keen sense of the ambiguity of every historic conflict, could be roused to a patriotic enthusiasm sufficient to counter the fanatical commitments on the other side.

The question before us in this chapter, then, is how Christian realism developed from a pessimistic, critical analysis of the contending forces in American society to a way of understanding government and politics that motivated people to struggle for democracy and justice. If *The Nature and Destiny of Man* provided Christian realism with more solid theological foundations, Niebuhr's work during and just after the Second World War made it a more articulate political philosophy.

The key work for this purpose was *The Children of Light and the Children of Darkness*, which appeared in late 1944. By then, it was far clearer than it had been during Niebuhr's lectures in Edinburgh that the Allies would win the war, but it was also becoming apparent to those who could look a little farther ahead that the defeat of Germany and Japan would not end the challenges that democracy would face on a global scale. The Soviet Union saw its own pattern of social economic organization emerging victorious and giving shape to the human future, and already in India, Algeria, and Syria, thoughtful observers could see the signs that the people who had come to the aid of their European colonizers during the war would have their own questions to ask about the future of democracy. Those who saw themselves as fighting to defend democracy as it had been understood and practiced in Europe and North America knew that they had an ongoing task before them. Niebuhr sought to integrate that defense into the Christian realism he had articulated for American society before the war.

At first, the title alone suggests that Niebuhr has forgotten something. The contrast between the "children of light" and the "children of darkness" seems to belong to the simple, unambiguous certainties of wartime, not to the realistic Christian ethics in which there is evil in every good and good in every evil. But there is a kind of Niebuhrian irony in the title itself. The children of light are not so unambiguously right as their designation would suggest, and the children of darkness—while they are wrong—are wrong in ways that are not entirely unknown among the believers in democracy. The clearer statement of Niebuhr's point is not the stark contrast of the title, but the lengthy description in the subtitle: "A Vindication of Democracy and a Critique of Its Traditional Defense."

Those who expect to be told why they are right and their enemies are wrong should not look here. They are more likely to learn that the reasons they thought they were right are the wrong reasons.

So, how does a Christian realist defend democracy? As with so many other issues, the argument begins with human nature. Both democracy and its enemies share human finitude, and both deal with the resulting anxiety by using power to protect themselves from their neighbors and by generating systems of ideas that justify this power and reassure them of their own invulnerability. The dynamics that Niebuhr traced in the first volume of *Nature and Destiny* are universally human, and the doctrine of original sin does not sort people out according to their political loyalties.

> Through it one may understand that no matter how wide the perspectives which the human mind may reach, how broad the loyalties which the human imagination may conceive, how universal the community which human statecraft may organize, or how pure the aspirations of the saintliest idealists may be, there is no level of human moral or social achievement in which there is not some corruption of inordinate self-love. [2]

The difference between the children of light and the children of darkness is not the difference between those who love themselves and those who do not. Loving self, rather than God and the neighbor, is the universal human condition. It is important to understand from the outset that democracy is no remedy for this fault. This is another of those realities that political realism must acknowledge, but should not expect to correct.

The difference between the children of light and the children of darkness comes in two basically different ways that people view the political problem that the reality of human nature poses. The children of darkness "know no law beyond their will and interest." [3] They look at the realities of self-interest and power that shape politics and international relations and conclude that this is all there is. Law, politics, and diplomacy have no purpose beyond security and success for themselves and their communities.

To be sure, the children of darkness may speak movingly of sacrifices for the people, or the party, or the faith. They may even be quite willing to sacrifice themselves as individuals for these causes. But the readiness to sacrifice always culminates in some group with which their own interest is totally identified, set against another group or groups who are the enemies who seek to destroy us, or who are the inferior races and nations who corrupt our purity and sap our strength. For the children of darkness, the idea that my people, party, or faith might make a sacrifice in the interest of some larger good is not just wrong. It is meaningless. There is nothing beyond to which such a sacrifice might be made.

Because of the limited horizon to their moral universe, Niebuhr also calls these children of darkness "moral cynics." [4] He does not mean by this that all of them have a snide, dismissive attitude toward moral ideas. Some of these children of darkness may be dewy-eyed idealists, but every ideal in the end refers back to the interests and power of the group where their commitments are centered. Nor is Niebuhr entirely unsympathetic to these cynical children of darkness. He recognizes that every realist runs the risk of becoming one of them. It is a short step from believing, as the realist does, that we cannot understand politics without understanding self-interest and power to believing, with the moral cynic, that self-interest and power are all there is. Become too consistent in your realism, and self-interest will not only be your clue to understanding politics. It will also become your guide to political choice. At that juncture, it will make little difference whether you continue to dismiss those who appeal to justice, truth, and goodness with a cynical question—What does *that* mean?—or whether you make up a new moral language in which the victory of your interests over your enemies simply is the truth toward which all history is pointing. You will still be one of the children of darkness. The political activist who can speak to three different audiences, appealing now to religion, then to racial identity, and at a third time to concerns about national security, all in an effort to "energize the base" and without believing in any of the messages, may seem to be a very different person from the cheering members of the audience who believe each speech and are energized by it; but the children of light are not distinguished from the children of darkness by their sincerity. Moral cynics know no law beyond their will and interest, even when they sincerely believe the idealistic terms in which they present their claims. Christian political realists understand the moral cynics, both the sincere and the insincere ones, but they must take care not to become one of them.

In the larger framework of Niebuhr's theology, it seems clear that the children of darkness do not believe in divine judgment and thus cannot inhabit the meaningful universe that divine judgment reveals. What is missing from their understanding of human nature is the freedom in which the self transcends itself by indeterminate degrees, and the understanding of judgment in which each level of commitment both affirms and negates those that have preceded it. [5] Those whose only law is self-interest locate that interest someplace—in themselves, if their interests are particularly narrow, or perhaps in a nation, a political movement, or a religious tradition, if their interests are broader. In any case, because this interest is the only law, it cannot affirm those parts of the self that lie below it. If the state or the party is the focus of self-interest, the self has no meaning apart from the state and must be sacrificed to the state when necessary. This does not contradict Niebuhr's analytical claim that self-interest is the only law for the children of darkness. It simply specifies where the interests of the self that are regarded as genuine are located. More important, because this interest is the only law, it cannot rise above itself to see its own limitations. The idea of a judgment in which the state or the party is partly affirmed and partly condemned is impossible, in contrast to the prophetic faith in which just such a judgment is anticipated for every new system or scheme of justice in which the self tries to locate its interests.

Niebuhr is not trying in *The Children of Light and the Children of Darkness* to distinguish the two groups on the basis of their religious beliefs, but it seems clear that we require his understanding of divine judgment to make sense of the difference between them. Whatever beliefs they might hold about God and human destiny, the children of darkness conduct their political lives as though there were no judgment of the sort that Niebuhr describes in the second volume of *Nature and Destiny*. For these moral cynics, there can be no ambiguity about their interests, no mixture of good and evil in whatever it is they make the center of their loyalties. Writing in 1944, Niebuhr saw Nazis and Fascists, the nationalist and racist movements in Germany and Italy, as the primary examples of the children of darkness in his day. No doubt he would have included the militarism, racial pride, and nationalism of Imperial Japan on the list, too, but he was primarily concerned with European culture and the distortions of Christian faith that helped shape Fascism and Nazism.

Six decades later, we must be careful not to confine Niebuhr's children of darkness too closely to Nazis and Fascists, about whom he was most concerned, lest we get the idea that the problem disappeared with the end of the Second World War. Of course, racist and nationalist ideas continue to play a role at the extremes of European politics, but our more serious concerns today are with forms of nationalism that have developed in reaction to the globalization of commerce and the spread of Western popular culture. In these movements, language, ethnic identity, traditional culture, religion, or some combination of these become elements in a center of loyalty that demands complete allegiance from those who are part of the group, requiring them to sacrifice any aspects of their own identity that have been absorbed from the global culture and to surrender any aspirations that are inconsistent with tradition. Women may be limited to traditional roles, for example; or multinational corporations and those who work for them may become targets of protest, sometimes violent.

Identifying the children of darkness is more complicated today, because we understand that many of these nationalist, racist, or fundamentalist movements have developed from concerns about economic exploitation and the erosion of cultural resources brought about by rapid Westernization. When we consider all the facts about them and all the forces that brought them into being, we find in these movements the ambiguous mix of good and evil that a Christian realist expects to find in any political group. However, the children of darkness cannot be identified by the truth or untruth of their claims any more than they can be identified by the sincerity of their speeches. Some of them are cynics who build support by repeating popular ideas that they do not believe, and some are convinced of the truth of everything they say. Some fabricate conspiracies and plots to justify their hatreds, as the Nazis invented Zionist plans for world domination. Others are victims of real injustice. What makes them children of darkness is the claim to an unambiguous purity that cannot be judged from any other perspective. Nor should we suppose that they are found only in nations and movements that reject democracy. The children of darkness are often eager to have democratic government as long as citizenship is restricted to the right kind of people.

If the children of darkness reject any appeals to the good, the right, or to God that do not unambiguously support their own claims, the children of light, by contrast, "seek to bring self-interest under the discipline of a more universal law and in harmony with a more universal good."[6] It is important to note that this discipline involves more than having a larger and more universal group. The children of darkness might be as small as a group of corrupt executives, plundering a corporation for their own profit, or as large as an international movement that attaches itself to a global religion. What is important is that once they have found a justification for their claims, judgment stops. What distinguishes the children of light is their readiness to accept evaluation in terms that transcend self-interest, and to continue that evaluation with the indeterminate transcendence of self that human freedom requires. The possibility of a more universal law and a more universal good is implicit in every law and every good we define, just as the law of love reveals the possibility of a still more complete justice every time we think we have created a new system of justice that resolves the problems of the old one.

Thus, we need the ideas of justice and judgment that Niebuhr develops in the second part of *Nature and Destiny*, both to understand the children of light and to identify the children of darkness. The children of light understand their place in history in terms very similar to those for whom the prophetic tradition leads to the expectation of a Christ. For them, moral meaning is not dependent on either historical triumph or the nobility of tragic failure.[7] It is just this similarity between "the discipline of a more universal law" and the meaning of divine judgment that creates the irony in Niebuhr's title. The children of light, because they know that their self-interest is not the highest law, know that they can never indulge in the kind of self-justification and self-glorification that marks the political rhetoric of the children of darkness. Those who claim to be children of light thus reveal that they are children of darkness, while the children of light know that pure good and pure evil do not exist in history.

This does not mean that the distinction between those who know no law beyond self-interest and those who subject self-interest to the discipline of a more universal law is unimportant. It means that democracy cannot be vindicated by its claims to moral purity or its connections to religious truth. Niebuhr is in fact little interested in *The Children of Light and the Children of Darkness* in whether democracy rests on religious beliefs, but he remains very concerned to identify those who are children of light in the specific, practical sense that he intends here. They are people who subject their political and personal choices to a moral judgment that is not based on immediate expectations of success. They are people who believe that self-interest is subject to a more universal law, and that it is possible, in some limited way, for those who understand this to make that more universal law effective in their political life.

Niebuhr's account of how history has meaning in *Nature and Destiny* would seem to imply that these children of light must share the prophetic faith, at least implicitly. Given the high failure rate of moral endeavors within history, following a more universal law and a higher good does not make much sense without the divine judgment that gives order to the unpredictable events of history. But it becomes clear in *The Children of Light and the Children of Darkness* that not all of the children of light understand this. There are some Marxists among the children of light, though not, presumably, the Stalinists who exploit Marx's ideas to establish themselves as the new ruling class in Russia. [8] Indeed, Niebuhr locates the children of light primarily among those who, like the Marxists, share an understanding of history that grows from the Enlightenment. This new age of reason began in Europe in the late seventeenth century, and marked the beginnings of modern, secular societies. Niebuhr, however, sees a continuing influence of Christianity in the way Enlightenment thinkers regard history as meaningful and expect progress toward a society that is more rational and more moral. In this, they differ from mystics, Platonic philosophers, and Buddhists (as Niebuhr understands Buddhism). These Enlightenment children of light also differ among themselves. For some, like Kant, reason provides the more universal law by which self-interest is limited. For the Marxists, the limit is built into the historical process itself. The capitalists' pursuit of self-interest generates so many contradictions that the system they set out to preserve eventually destroys itself. [9] These differences are important, but Niebuhr also sees an underlying unity in the secularized accounts of meaningful history offered by Enlightenment political thinkers from, say, John Locke (1632–1704) to Karl Marx (1818–1883).

Because of their influence on modern political thought, these Enlightenment philosophers and their followers may be the most influential children of light in the modern world. However, they are certainly not alone. Catholic moral theologians who evaluate the claims of self-interest through the tradition of natural law, which goes back to Thomas Aquinas and to Aristotle, are also children of light. So, too, are important Protestant theologians in the tradition of Martin Luther, though they are far more pessimistic than the Enlightenment thinkers about the moral law providing effective limits on self-interest. As we will see, Niebuhr thought their pessimism was largely correct, and these Protestants are from his point of view the most realistic of the children of light.

Still, it is the Enlightenment philosophers who gave us the traditional defense of liberal democracy that most interest Reinhold Niebuhr in his analysis of the global conflict that was underway as he wrote in 1944. Their optimism about our human capacity for moral judgment made it possible to leave the world of kings who claimed divine authority and local barons who ruled in their own interest and to envision government by the people themselves, but their failure to see the residual power of self-interest, even among the children of light, put their achievements at risk from the remorseless self-assertion of the children of darkness.

Niebuhr's focus on the political legacy of the Enlightenment makes it a little difficult for us to identify just who should be counted among the children of light today. At the beginning of the twenty-first century, some of the most important questions about democracy have to do with how it works in non-Western cultures that do not share the heritage of the Enlightenment. Is it necessary first to become modern, Western, and secular in order to have a successful democracy? Or does democracy, despite its Western, Enlightenment history, rest on some basic principles that people from a variety of cultures and religions can affirm and still retain their distinctive, non-Western identities?[10] Does every system of government that brings self-interest under the discipline of a higher law have to look something like modern democracy? Or could we imagine people living by quite a different set of rules from those that prevail in a democracy and still think of them as children of light?

Those questions have an urgency for us today that they could not have for Niebuhr, making the case for democracy against Fascism and Nazism, and we will not be able to develop complete answers to them here. Our task is to understand clearly how Niebuhr's defense of democracy differs from the Enlightenment arguments for it. Further reflection might then suggest new ways for us to think about the possibilities for democracy today, so that we recognize all of the children of light who might become our partners and do not mistake any of them for the children of darkness whom we must oppose.

The problem with the children of light that most concerned Niebuhr was their optimism and their confidence in the power of democratic ideas to transform self-interested politics. Like the idealistic Christians who regard Jesus' law of love as a simple historical possibility, which they and their communities could follow if they just tried hard enough, modern democracy is sentimental. "It has an easy solution for the problem of anarchy and chaos on both the national and the international level of community, because of its fatuous and superficial view of man."[11] The problem, in short, is that most of the children of light are foolish. They think that most people really want to pursue the general good and can easily moderate their pursuit of self-interest, so they expect more from democratic politics than it usually can deliver, and they have a hard time recognizing the children of darkness when they see them.

A typical vindication of democracy thus begins with the idea that the people should rule themselves because they can do a better job of it than kings or dictators. Ordinary people, who are mostly children of light, know what they want, and while they will react desperately if they lack the means of survival, when they have a reasonable amount of the things they want, they will live peaceably with their neighbors and make the necessary sacrifices for the common good.

This is an ideal that can be traced back to Thomas Jefferson's ideal of a republic composed of prosperous, independent farmers who would provide for their

own welfare and the well-being of their families while living together in harmony. It is only when tyrants deprive them of their rights or stir them up to go
to war against other people that they fail to keep the peace. This "social idealism
which informs our democratic civilisation," Niebuhr writes, "had a touching
faith in the possibility of achieving a simple harmony between self-interest and
the general welfare on every level." [12] After wiping away a sentimental tear of
admiration for these democratic people, however, we need to come to a realistic
recognition that they do not exist. Most people are more self-interested than
that. They demand a reasonable accommodation for their own needs and desires,
and given what they say they need, they come up with good reasons why they
should have even more. They do not achieve a moderate self-sufficiency and
then devote all their energies to the common good.

So the assumption that lies at the heart of the traditional defense of democracy, which is that people have moderate desires and will live at peace with one
another if they are given the chance to do it, is false. Not only that, it is dangerous, because if we make false assumptions about how people will act, democracy will fail; and people will then be easily persuaded to follow dictators. Hitler's
exploitation of the political opportunities created by the failure of the Weimar
Republic was an example much on the minds of Niebuhr's generation.

A more realistic vindication of democracy would begin with the realization
that the moral cynics among the children of darkness understand an important
truth: people will pursue their own interest at the expense of the general welfare
whenever they are given the chance. This does not mean, as the cynics suppose
it does, that the moral law is irrelevant. But it does mean that we cannot expect
people to limit their pursuit of self-interest without some restraint. As Luther
observed, when the sheep and wolves are commanded to live together in peace,
the sheep will obey, but they will not live very long. [13]

So we cannot defend democracy with the simple idea that dictatorships
employ coercion to restrain their people and democracies do not. Democracy,
too, requires a strong government capable of providing order and restraining evil.
Instead of lending their support to sentimental illusions about democracy,
Christians need to participate in these efforts to maintain internal order and
external security. This theme, too, has deep roots in theology, in Augustine's portrait of the reluctant judge who takes up out of public necessity the task of
restraining evil, and in Luther's advice to Christians that "if you see that there is
a lack of hangmen, constables, judges, lords, or princes, and you find that you are
qualified, you should offer your services and seek the position, that the essential
governmental authority may not be despised and become enfeebled or perish." [14]
Niebuhr recalls these points at which Protestant theology was more realistic
about human nature than the Enlightenment thinking that followed, but he is
no doubt also thinking of the strong prewar commitment to pacifism shared by
many American pastors and theologians of his generation. Niebuhr respected
pacifism as part of the historic witness of the church, but he had no doubt that

the responsible choice for Christians in the Western democracies during the Second World War was to offer their services in whatever way would support their governments against their enemies, even if that involved them in the violence that was necessarily part of the war effort. [15]

Realistic understanding of any government has to begin with this measure of power and coercion that must be in the hands of the authorities if self-interested human nature is to be held to a workable system of cooperation that will provide the order and security that any society requires. To suppose that a democracy can dispense with power is dangerous to the citizens, who will thereby be exposed to those who will expand their own power at the expense of others unless they are prevented from doing so, and dangerous to the democracy itself, which is likely to be rejected when people find that it cannot provide order.

If Enlightenment idealists mistakenly think that democracy can ignore the requirements of order, classical political realists like Luther or Thomas Hobbes have been apt to think of democracy as a luxury, an indulgence to be regarded with suspicion, because it might undermine the commitment to order. Neither group is able to provide a successful argument for democracy, although the traditional defense has relied heavily on Enlightenment idealism.

Niebuhr's realistic case for democracy, however, begins by pointing out that the classical political realists are not quite consistent in their argument for a strong political authority. We need authority because people will follow their self-interest instead of pursuing the general good every time, unless some power is present to prevent it. But the question Niebuhr wants to ask is, "Who prevents the rulers from pursuing self-interest?" The question is particularly acute if you begin with Niebuhr's assessment of human nature, which suggests that the rulers will develop a set of ideas to explain why their self-interest is good for everybody and that, in the end, it is the rulers themselves who are apt to believe those ideas most sincerely. The only way to be a consistent realist, then, is to avoid Luther's too-consistent pessimism and ask instead what we might do to limit the power of the rulers. At that point, a democratic system that puts power over the rulers in the hands of the people begins to make sense. The consistent argument for democracy is that every center of power needs to be limited by some other, alternative center of power. If the power to use force and the majesty of the law are concentrated in the hands of a few rulers, the power to choose those rulers or dismiss them needs to be widely dispersed among the people.

It turns out, then, that a plausible defense of democracy begins by understanding that democracy is a system of coercion. Democracy is not a system in which everybody is set free for life, liberty, and the pursuit of happiness. Democracy is a system of constraint in which mutual agreements establish systems of checks and balances that control the pursuit of self-interest, including the pursuit of self-interest by those who are in control of the government. "All political justice is achieved by coercing the anarchy of collective self-interest into some kind of decent order by the most attainable balance of power," Niebuhr wrote. [16] That explains the success of the modern liberal democracies better than their own optimistic political theories, and Niebuhr increasingly believed that an attainable balance of power would be the key to peace amidst the continuing conflicts of the postwar world.

This does not reduce the search for justice to an illusion. Human beings do have a limited, real capacity to transcend their self-interest and imagine new relationships that would serve everyone better than the present tensions and conflicts. But they will never get to the point of seeking justice unless they are constrained by an order that is established by power. A balance of power, "once achieved, can be stabilized, embellished, and even, on occasion, perfected by more purely moral considerations. But there has never been a scheme of justice in history which did not have a balance of power at its foundation." [17]

If the children of darkness were right, justice would be impossible. There would be no conception of a higher standard by which to measure our momentary achievements of justice, and self-interest would provide only a measure of improvement. The future is better than the past if it gets us more of what we want. It is pointless to deny that we all do think about history in that way at times, but it is untrue to say that is the only way we think about it.

If the foolish children of light were right, justice would be inevitable. Once people are set free to pursue their self-interest as they see it, they will do so in moderation and with a proper concern for the good of the whole community. We would not have to worry about wars or dictatorships, because people who can pursue their self-interest freely will do so peaceably, and they will rule each other wisely. This is an attractive vision, and it returns periodically to dominate American perceptions of our own politics and our role in the world. But it underestimates the power of self-interest and the tendency of power to seek more power. The reason we need democracy is that we have to give so much power to the people and institutions who supply the necessary order. Once they have power, we can be sure we will have order; but we cannot hope for justice unless there are democratic limits on their power.

Niebuhr's realism tries to maintain the right relationship between the cynical falsehood that makes justice impossible and the foolish half-truth that makes justice inevitable. He summarized the true relationship between politics, ethics, and human nature, as he understood it, in one of his most famous sentences, in the foreword to *The Children of Light and the Children of Darkness*: "Man's capacity for justice makes democracy possible; but man's inclination to injustice makes democracy necessary." [18] In those words, the prophetic search for justice and realistic politics come together.

Questions for Reflection

1. Who are the children of light and the children of darkness? Which persons or groups did Niebuhr regard as representative of each in his own time? Are you

surprised by any whom he includes among the children of light or the children of darkness?

2. Why does Niebuhr regard both Marxists and Enlightenment political philosophers as "foolish children of light"? How are their political ideas different, and what does Niebuhr think that they nevertheless have in common?

3. What is the problem with the traditional defense of democracy? What alternative explanation does Niebuhr offer to show that democracy is a good way to organize a political system?

CHAPTER FIVE

FAITH AND HISTORY

The years after the Second World War marked the high point of Reinhold Niebuhr's activity and influence. In contrast to the wave of pacifist idealism that swept over American Protestantism in reaction to the First World War, Christians who considered the situation in the late 1940s recognized quickly that they would continue to live in a dangerous and divided world. Niebuhr and the young Christian realists had worked hard to dispel the illusions of the 1920s. Two decades later, their ideas had proved their staying power; and church leaders, politicians, and diplomats resonated with the Christian realists' warning that justice and peace are approximations to be sustained by power, rather than goals that human communities naturally seek.

Niebuhr himself seemed to be everywhere in those years—lecturing; preaching; teaching; corresponding with cultural, judicial, and religious leaders; advising politicians and State Department officials—but his ideas were even more ubiquitous than he was. His themes and phrases showed up in countless sermons, with or without acknowledgment. Political scientists and commentators praised his insights and echoed his analyses of American politics and world events. Even his critics among the secular philosophers acknowledged that his ideas about original sin and human nature had an important place in contemporary life and thought. [1]

Niebuhr's activities slowed after he suffered a stroke in 1952, but by then, much of his realism about politics and human nature had become received public wisdom: Justice at home and peace abroad depend on maintaining a balance of power, rather than planning to triumph over our enemies. The strength of democracy lies in its capacity for self-criticism. The weakness of Communism is the ideological rigidity that places its leaders above judgment.

No one book summarizes Niebuhr's insights for this period the way that *Moral Man and Immoral Society* spoke to the 1930s or *The Children of Light and the*

47

Children of Darkness gave a realistic interpretation of the conflict with totalitarianism. Many of the relevant themes, however, appear in *Faith and History*, [2] a collection of lectures and essays that returns from the immediate problems of politics and Cold War diplomacy to the broad questions of whether history has a meaning and how our moral lives relate to divine transcendence. Here, as in *Nature and Destiny*, Niebuhr suggests that although historical events are susceptible to divine judgment, they provide no final vindication of Christian faith. The law of love is a relevant ideal, but no direct line can be drawn from the ethics of Jesus to the requirements of responsible choice.

Niebuhr's understanding of responsibility suggested what his personality in any case required: a restless ranging across all fields of knowledge and systems of thought to find clues to policies that could contribute to approximate justice while taking full account of the realities of power and self-interest. Even though at this distance we tend to see Niebuhr standing almost alone, articulating his insights out of his own theology, he formed his ideas in vigorous debate, and he was often most clear about his own position when stating his disagreements with those who had other ideas. In this chapter, we want to understand Christian realism of the Cold War years through some of these debates and disagreements. Only a few of the multitude of thinkers who influenced Niebuhr can be considered, and we will concentrate on those whose ideas appear most important from our perspective, rather than on those with whom he had the closest personal relationships.

Karl Barth was a figure whom Niebuhr both admired and criticized throughout their long careers. [3] Barth wanted to turn Christians away from the illusions of progress and restore a more theological understanding of human possibilities. He saw a rediscovery of the biblical world of sin and grace as central to that purpose. Other types of knowledge and methods of study were beside the point. Even the methods of biblical study were a distraction, if they interfered with the work of the Spirit by which the words of the biblical text become the Word of God for us.

At the outset, Niebuhr believed that he and Barth shared the same goal, but Niebuhr was skeptical that American Protestants could find direction solely by rediscovering the world of the Bible. Americans had illusions about the Bible, as well as illusions about progress. Sometimes the two sets of illusions were closely related. If the objective is to reintroduce a distinctive biblical viewpoint, Americans would grasp that better by learning more about the philosophies and faiths that take a different view, as Niebuhr tried to instruct them in *Nature and Destiny*.

What Niebuhr admired most about Barth was his steadfast resistance to Hitler and to the Nazi reinterpretation of Christianity behind the "German Christian" movement of the 1930s. It was Barth's theological leadership that rallied pastors and laypeople to the Confessing Church, which sought to maintain the integrity of theology and church governance against Nazi demands that the church take a subordinate role in the new National Socialist state. Precisely because of this leadership, however, Barth was expelled from Germany to his native Switzerland in 1935, and both he and Niebuhr observed the disastrous fate of Germany and its churches from a distance.

Barth's criticism of both Protestant liberalism and the Nazi distortions of Christianity rested on a firm insistence that the kingdom of God cannot be identified with any movement or historical development, but stands in judgment on all of them. Niebuhr would have agreed, of course, but he began to think that Barth's strong critical attitude was not sufficiently balanced by a responsible attitude, which could make discriminating choices among the alternatives to the great evil that he deplored. This became more important after the war, when Christians had to participate in the restoration of democratic government in Europe, and especially as the churches had to respond to the imposition of Communist rule in the states of Eastern Europe. Barth had thought of himself before the war as a Christian socialist, but he shared none of Niebuhr's enthusiasm for socialist politics. At the same time, Barth was reluctant to make a theological judgment against Communist policies, even when these turned repressive and began to involve persecution of the churches. By 1948, when the World Council of Churches held its first Assembly in Amsterdam, Niebuhr concluded that Barth's theology was not sufficient for the choices that would have to be made in the new, postwar world. The Confessing Church had been a powerful witness, Niebuhr agreed. "But perhaps this theology is constructed too much for the great crises of history. It seems to have no guidance for a Christian statesman for our day. It can fight the devil if he shows both horns and both cloven feet. But it refuses to make discriminating judgments about good and evil if the evil shows only one horn or the half of a cloven foot." [4]

Niebuhr became more insistent on the importance of these discriminating judgments as his own opposition to Communism strengthened. He was especially disturbed by Barth's failure to condemn the Russian invasion of Hungary in 1956. The ultimate judgment of God, for Barth, rendered changes of regime and government insignificant. He did not want to defend Communism, but he refused to give theological significance to what he regarded as purely political developments. Niebuhr's entire work from *An Interpretation of Christian Ethics* onward had, by contrast, been devoted to establishing the relevance of God's ultimate judgment to concrete political choices.

Niebuhr's disagreement with Barth over Christian responsibility did not necessarily move him closer to other European theologians who had been Barth's persistent critics. In contrast to Barth's insistence that Christian ethics must respond only to the Word of God, Emil Brunner had argued for a theology that came much closer to Niebuhr's Christian realism, finding guidance for specific moral choices not only in biblical theology, but also in the "orders of creation." [5] These orders were the enduring structures of work, family, church, culture, and government through which the will of God might be found by examining the ways that God has provided to sustain and order human life. For Niebuhr, this idea of a moral order known in nature did not give sufficient attention to the freedom from natural constraints that is also part of human life. In addition, the way that self-interest distorts every human understanding makes it particularly likely that people in power will systematically interpret the requirements of the created order in ways that reinforce existing hierarchies and inequalities. To the slaveowner, slavery always seems part of the order that God has provided for organizing human work. Thus, despite the large role that human nature plays in Niebuhr's own political understanding, he remained reluctant to identify his thinking too closely with Brunner's ideas, or with any of the other ways that theology used the created order to shape ethics. When it came to making practical political judgments, his skepticism about how self-interest distorts our perception of what is "natural" outweighed his conviction that human nature shapes the life of human communities. Those who move directly from human nature to moral norms, Niebuhr thought, will almost always confuse what is familiar and what fits their own prejudices with the order of creation.

The most important of those traditions linking the created, natural order and the imperatives of ethics was Catholic teaching on natural law. [6] Beginning from the theology of Thomas Aquinas, who linked natural, divine, and human law in a great system of moral order dependent on the eternal law of God, Catholic theologians drew rules for both personal and political life from the goals of human actions that could be seen in the order of nature. Sexual ethics followed from the purpose of procreation. Rules for marriage, family life, and education followed from the goal of raising and nurturing children. Even the fundamental rules of labor and politics followed from the natural tendency of human beings to live together in organized communities.

Like most Protestant theologians of his generation, Niebuhr acquired limited knowledge of details and recent developments in this tradition during his education, and his early works echoed standard Protestant criticisms: The corruption of sin undermines our ability to know the requirements of natural justice. Catholic theory "speaks of an original righteousness which was lost in the Fall and a natural justice which remains uncorrupted by the Fall. This distinction obscures the complex relation of human freedom to all of man's natural functions, and the consequent involvement of all 'natural' or 'rational' standards and norms in sin." [7] As a result, the natural law tradition often fails to recognize demands for justice that contradict prevailing social practices, while it transforms a particular set of social relationships that prevailed in the feudal, agrarian world of the Middle Ages into a fixed order of nature.

Recent work in Catholic moral theology, however, did not entirely conform to this Protestant stereotype. John Courtney Murray, a Jesuit theologian who explored issues of church and state from a Catholic perspective, drew attention to an American "public consensus" that provided a moral foundation for law and politics and shared many assumptions with the natural law tradition. In ways that historians focused on the Enlightenment often overlook, Murray argued, the natural law tradition has provided moral authority for American democracy. At the same time, the democratic experience has transformed our understanding of the requirements of natural law. [8] In Murray's hands, natural law provided a way to see the connections between ancient Roman law, Christian theology, English common law, and constitutional democracy. Interestingly, Rabbi Robert Gordis applied the biblical tradition to American politics in much the same way from a Jewish perspective. [9]

Clearly, this was not Catholic natural law as Niebuhr expected to find it, stuck in the world of Thomas Aquinas, isolated from other discussions, and unconnected to the political life of a democratic society. In fact, Murray's purposes were much the same as Niebuhr's in *The Children of Light and the Children of Darkness*. Murray, too, wanted to vindicate democracy against its critics. In his case, the critics were conservative Catholics who equated the separation of church and state with a secular rejection of religion and saw democratic pluralism as a threat to Catholic truth. Likewise, Murray thought that the traditional defense of democracy, grounded in Enlightenment optimism and individualism, could not provide the response that was needed. Instead, he argued that democratic reliance on reasoned argument and public consensus originate in the older political and legal norms of natural law. This meant that conservative Catholics had to rethink their rejection of American democracy, but it also implied that American secularists had to revise their understanding of Catholicism as anti-democratic. All of this acquired practical political importance when a Catholic, John F. Kennedy, became the Democratic presidential candidate in 1960, but Murray had been arguing the case in more technical theological terms—and against serious criticism from other Catholics—for more than a decade before that. At one point, he was forbidden by authorities in Rome to publish his writings on church and state, but he persisted in his basic principles, and the idea of religious freedom that he saw as central to human dignity won recognition as part of Catholic teaching at the Second Vatican Council. [10]

Niebuhr and Murray met on several occasions, including extended discussions at the Center for the Study of Democratic Institutions, which was an important meeting ground for political and intellectual leaders in the early 1960s. [11] There is more evidence that Murray read Niebuhr than vice versa, but the two could hardly have missed the parallels between their roles in Catholic and Protestant religious life. Each was leading his church into a more active role in American politics, seeking a higher justice on basic issues facing the nation, and providing a defense of America's role in the Cold War that went beyond conventional patriotism.

They disagreed sharply, nevertheless, over natural law. Niebuhr continued to mistrust the formulations of general moral principles that Murray thought were essential for moral reasoning, while Murray thought that Protestant ethics was beset by fuzzy thinking and what he called "ambiguism." Murray never specifically charged Niebuhr with these failings in print, but there is little doubt whom he had in mind in this passage:

> The proper bafflers are the ambiguists. Their flashes of insight are frequent enough; but in the end the fog closes down. They are great ones for the facts, against the fundamentalists, and great ones for "conscience," against the cynics. They insist on the values of pragmatism against the absolutists; but they resent the suggestion that they push pragmatism to the point of a relativism of moral values. [12]

At this point, Murray's criticism of Niebuhr has a certain similarity to Niebuhr's criticism of Barth. The emphasis on theological integrity results in a failure of ethics. Of course, Murray can hardly say that Niebuhr is unwilling to make judgments about specific political events, which is the problem Niebuhr had with Barth's theology. Niebuhr's works are full of moral judgments. Murray's complaint is that Niebuhr is unwilling to make a moral argument. "My main difficulty," Murray writes, "is that I never know what, in their argument, is fact and what is moral category (surely there is a difference), or where the process of history ends and the moral order begins (surely there must be such a point)." [13]

Niebuhr would reject the critical edge, but he might admit that Murray has captured something important about how a Christian realist thinks. The complex strategies by which human freedom deals with the realities of history cannot be reduced to fixed moral principles, but the constancy of human nature, observed over a long enough history, yields broad generalizations, which it is unwise to ignore. We can never be sure that history will follow the course that we project, but we can make judgments about the possibilities based on experience. When events turn out contrary to expectations, as they often will, it is because the ironies of history make it impossible to turn historical analysis into a law of historical development. Call this "ambiguism," if you will. For Niebuhr, it is both historical process *and* moral order. Barth is as wrong to exclude this experience from his theological judgments as Murray is to think that it can be reduced to principles of natural law.

Niebuhr does not think of moral judgments in terms of fixed principles from which particular moral judgments can be derived. He views history as a balance between contending forces, so that moral judgments are best cast in the form of extended discussions of where that balance now lies and the direction in which it is tending. Applying absolute distinctions between right and wrong to these large historical developments is often impossible and usually unhelpful for making concrete political choices.

Thus, when Niebuhr assesses the demands for justice that are such a common feature of contemporary politics, he sets them in the context of the whole history of government going back to the empires of Egypt and Babylon. What distinguishes modern government from its ancient roots is that its legitimacy is tied to justice, and not only to order. Modern governments cannot retain power without at least pretending to provide justice, in contrast to premodern systems that rested on the ruler's inherited authority or divine authorization. The nature of the justice sought, however, changes over time. Today, demands for justice are primarily demands for greater equality—for more equal distribution of wealth, more equal status as citizens, or more equal treatment of racial and religious minorities. But it was not always so. At the beginning of modern Western democracy, the demand for justice was primarily a demand for greater liberty—for more freedom from distant colonial powers, free markets, lower taxes, and more representative government. No single meaning of justice can be derived from these diverse movements and demands, and no set of rules would allow us to say with certainty whether a particular economic or political order is just. The modern idea of justice is simply what these demands have made of it.

Nevertheless, some important generalizations are possible. Most obviously, the demand for justice tends to shift back and forth between liberty and equality. Liberty and equality are not unrelated concepts. A successful demand for one tends to set the conditions for greater demands for the other. The demand for liberty introduces Jeffersonian democracy, under which liberty eventually produces intolerable inequalities of wealth and power, so that reforms from the Progressive era through the New Deal introduce controls and constraints that make for greater economic and political equality. History suggests, then, that liberty and equality are "regulative principles" of justice. Judgments about justice at a particular point in time turn on how the prevailing equilibrium between liberty and equality has come about, and on the direction in which events seem to be moving, toward greater liberty or greater equality.

We can formulate theories about this shifting equilibrium, but "our political thought always lags behind our practice. Our performance is wiser than our theory; and we are more virtuous than we claim to be." [14] That last thought, surely, is an odd one for a Christian realist. Perhaps what Niebuhr means is that we are more virtuous than we would appear to be when measured against the natural law theorist's absolute moral standards. In any case, Niebuhr's Christian realism makes the strong claim that its judgments follow the complexities of history more closely than a more rigorous pattern of argument could do. Niebuhr makes more use of all the facts than Barth's theology, and he is more able to identify the evil in every good and the good in every evil than Murray's natural law.

What Niebuhr perhaps does not see so clearly is the way this his own thinking is a kind of natural law theory. His judgments depend on a theologically informed understanding of human nature, just as Murray's natural law rests on the idea, which can be traced back to Thomas Aquinas, that there is a shared core of human reason that does not depend for knowledge on divine revelation and is not so affected by sin that it needs to rely on divine grace to grasp moral truth. Niebuhr's "ambiguism" is not so much an alternative to natural law thinking. It is an alternative view of natural law that follows from a different understanding of human nature. After taking a more ecumenical overview of modern Christian ethics, Paul Ramsey argued that Niebuhr is a natural law thinker despite himself. [15]

Niebuhr, however, shows no signs of yielding on this point. For him, the natural law simply is the legalistic version he finds in his reading of Catholic moral theology, and he is particularly concerned with the practical point that this legalism will not provide the flexibility that is necessary, if we are to preserve justice in a rapidly changing technological society. [16] The equilibrium between liberty and equality shifts too rapidly for fixed principles to be of much use in political discussions.

Niebuhr might appreciate the irony that principles drawn from natural law have become far more important in public discussions than he could have anticipated. While John F. Kennedy tried to separate his Catholic faith from his responsibilities as a political leader during his election campaign in 1960, subsequent decades have seen an increase in visible political participation not only by Catholic laity, but by their church's leadership as well. Principles drawn from natural law have been prominent in these developments. Cardinal Joseph Bernardin, the Archbishop of Chicago, for example, spoke and wrote about a "consistent ethic of life" that would apply a principle of respect for the human person to political decisions about war and peace, abortion, and capital punishment. [17] In the debates that preceded the U.S. invasion of Iraq in 2003, just war theory, formed historically in Catholic understandings of natural justice in armed conflict, provided an important framework by which both opponents and advocates of the war sought to justify their positions.

The irony comes in the fact that these recent discussions have been conducted with far more attention to the theological presuppositions of natural law than either Niebuhr or Murray would have expected. Murray believed that natural law doctrine provides a minimum of morality based on reason and independent of specifically Christian ideas about sin, pride, and human nature. That would be its contribution to a pluralistic political discussion, even though Catholics could affirm both the doctrine and the discussion on the basis of their religious convictions. Niebuhr understood that this was what natural law proposed to do, and he rejected natural law because he did not think that such a neat separation between faith and reason in the understanding of human nature was possible. In the years since Vatican II, however, Catholic theology itself has questioned the sharp distinction between "natural" humanity that can be known by reason and human nature as it is related to God. [18] The public discussion of natural law that Niebuhr did not expect has come to pass, but it is a discussion that has more of Niebuhr's "ambiguist" understanding of human nature than Murray would have allowed.

Niebuhr's reluctance to see principles alone as a sound basis for policy or for moral judgment may also have contributed to his increasing distance from the organized political work of the Protestant churches. Even before American entry into the Second World War, the Federal Council of Churches organized a commission to study the bases for a "just and durable" peace. Niebuhr participated in this work, along with many other religious and political leaders, including John Foster Dulles, who would later become U.S. secretary of state. The thirteen Guiding Principles that they issued reflected a consensus among the theologians and policymakers on the need for a stronger international organization than the failed League of Nations and a stronger system of international law, although the commission's compromises between moral idealism and political realism were not universally applauded. After the war, ecumenical leaders followed up on the commission's principles and other wartime studies by concentrating their attention on the emerging organization of the United Nations, and on making sure that its charter provided protections for human rights as well as a setting for diplomacy. [19] Niebuhr supported these developments, and the church leaders drew ideas from his work, but his personal involvement was limited.

Increasingly, he found his conversation partners among the political theorists and historians, rather than the theologians. Many of them were strongly influenced by Niebuhr's realism, and Hans Morgenthau saw analysis of self-interest and power as the starting point for a new, scientific approach to understanding international relations. The historian Arthur Schlesinger Jr. agreed with Niebuhr that the irony of history was an important corrective to those who saw the American story as a straightforward progress of virtue and enlightenment. When Charles Kegley and Robert Bretall prepared a volume of essays that assessed Niebuhr's contributions to religious, social, and political thought, the authors included philosophers, historians, and political scientists alongside the theologians. [20]

In these circles, talk centered more on the containment of Soviet power than on the moral evils of Communism, though Niebuhr would have insisted that a durable peace was also the objective of the political realists in the State Department, and that justice depended on American power as well as the principles of human rights. Characteristically, however, he also insisted that the paradoxes and contradictions held in tension in the Christian view of human nature cannot be confined to a fully consistent, scientific realism, [21] just as he had warned his theological colleagues a generation before against treating Jesus' love ethic as a simple historical possibility.

Not all secular thinkers found Niebuhr's realistic interpretation of Christianity so compatible with their own ways of thinking. Morton White was a philosopher who shared many of Niebuhr's political commitments and acknowledged his influence on intellectual leaders in many fields. In fact, the generation of realists who guided the government after the Second World War were, White said, so enamored of Niebuhr's understanding of human nature that they should have formed an organization called "atheists for Niebuhr." White, himself a historian of American thought, suggested that some of Niebuhr's intellectual influence also derived from pragmatism, which he absorbed in his early studies of William James, and from his general style of argument, which was empirical and not given to formal, logical structures. In that, Niebuhr had hit on a way of thinking widely shared among American intellectuals. What the "atheists for Niebuhr" overlooked, however, is that Niebuhr provided no arguments to back up his insights, apart from the theology on which his account of human nature rested. His convictions rested on faith, and the atheists surely were not going to follow him there.

From White's point of view, perhaps, this unmasking disqualifies Niebuhr as a genuine public intellectual, despite the fact that "he is a shrewd, courageous, and right-minded man on many political questions." [22] Niebuhr would not deny the theology, but he would defend his claim as a public intellectual on more pragmatic grounds. Ideas do not become public because they are certifiably uncontaminated by faith. They become public by providing coherence to more limited and fragmentary ideas that are widely shared among the diverse people who make up the public. Niebuhr would go on to say that this coherence falls far short of universal meaning. It simply makes sense of things to a lot of people who happen to be involved in the conversation, here and now. That "limited rational validation," however, is available to the truths of faith, too. [23]

In an unexpected way, then, Morton White's criticism of Niebuhr exactly parallels Karl Barth's. Both require that theological truths be isolated from everything else that we think we know. For Barth, the separation is necessary to prevent the illusions of the culture from contaminating the confession of faith. For White, it is necessary to prevent the paradoxes and irrationalities of faith from undermining the shared, rational beliefs on which social cooperation can be built. In neither case could theological ideas make much sense to those who do not share the faith behind them.

Niebuhr believes that neither our faith nor our reason are as pure as Barth and White require them to be. But he believes it for theological reasons. The human being who is both made in the image of God and a sinful, limited creature can neither grasp the reality of God perfectly nor rely solely on autonomous reason, entirely apart from God. If that is the reality of the human condition, we should not expect to understand it without the assistance of God's grace. But because it is the reality of the human condition, we should not think that possibilities and limitations that arise from this relationship to God will entirely escape anyone who looks carefully and honestly at human experience.

White and Barth share more than we might at first expect, and what they share sets them at odds with Niebuhr. But what sets Niebuhr at odds with White and Barth, he also shares with Murray and the natural law tradition, especially as that tradition has developed since Vatican II. Christian realism should not be defined solely by the way that it challenged the optimistic assumptions of American Protestantism at the beginning of the twentieth century, nor does it begin and end with Niebuhr's generation. Niebuhr was increasingly clear that

Christian realism has to be traced back at least as far as Augustine. Events at the end of his life and during the years immediately following his death would raise the question of whether this legacy has a future.

Questions for Reflection

1. How does Niebuhr differ with Karl Barth over the role of Christians in society? What specific events and historical developments led Niebuhr to criticize Barth?

2. What relationships have contemporary Catholic theologians established between church teaching and democracy? How do these ideas compare with Niebuhr's criticisms of historic formulations of natural law by Thomas Aquinas and others?

3. Why did Niebuhr increasingly seek his dialogue partners among philosophers and political thinkers? Did he expect his theological ideas to make specific and important contributions in those discussions?

CHAPTER SIX

CHRISTIAN REALISM: PLURALISTIC AND HOPEFUL

Reinhold Niebuhr lived through some dramatic changes in the world of events and in the world of ideas. In the 1930s, he confronted failing peace plans, economic problems, and racial unrest with a stark realism that ran counter to the optimism of American culture and the idealism of American religion. His insistence on the importance of power and the pervasive influence of self-interest startled those who were accustomed to making Christian love more immediately relevant to the solution of social problems, but his work laid the groundwork for a realistic defense of democracy during the Second World War, and his Christian realism provided moral direction for a generation of leaders who shaped politics and diplomacy for the harsh world of the Cold War and nuclear deterrence. The theologian whose grasp of events put him on the margins of acceptable theology in the early 1930s found himself two decades later at the center of a world of ideas that offered a way to understand what was happening in world events.

Then another set of changes challenged this Christian realist way of thinking. Growing nuclear arsenals led some to ask whether the balance of power between the United States and the Soviet Union was a moral, or even a workable, way to maintain world peace. Activists impatient for racial equality began to question whether the cautious balancing of nonviolent resistance against entrenched power was any more effective than the sentimental appeals to Christian love it was supposed to replace. Women who understood the importance of asserting themselves against economic and social subordination wondered why pride always had to be seen as a form of sin. In the years after Niebuhr's death in 1971, his realism seemed to have as many critics as it had in 1932 when *Moral Man and Immoral Society* first appeared. The world was changing, and new ideas—liberation theology, feminism, nuclear pacifism, and ecological activism—offered ways to understand the new realities. By the 1980s, it might have seemed that Reinhold Niebuhr's Christian realism had become a subject of interest mostly to historians.

Two decades later, another set of changes has reshaped the world of events. Superpower confrontation has been replaced by a new, less predictable threat of terrorism launched not from distant enemy nations, but by disaffected groups who may plan their aggression in the very cities they intend to attack. Military forces that effectively contained and deterred opposing armies prove less effective against insurgencies and armed political groups. Meanwhile, Internet images of global culture and political change hint at new realities that are still poorly understood. Europe has a common Parliament and an effective Court of Human Rights that can overrule national legislatures with centuries of sovereign power behind them. But Scotland, once again, has a Parliament, too. It meets in a building designed by a Spanish architect. Russia has a Parliament, perhaps its first effective one ever. It meets in a nondescript Soviet-era building in the center of Moscow. You might walk by it without knowing what it was. But you could not miss the familiar logos of the American fast food outlets in the neighborhood. This is not Reinhold Niebuhr's world.

Christian realism, however, is more than a series of astute observations that Reinhold Niebuhr made about the events of his time. Niebuhr believed that his analysis rested both on paying careful attention to the forces that were shaping contemporary events *and* on a biblical understanding of human nature and history that transcends its application to any one place or time. At the beginning of the twenty-first century, we are perhaps just far enough from Niebuhr's time that we can begin to employ that vision independently of his judgments about the events that he himself experienced.

The legacy of Niebuhr's Christian realism is not a specific set of policy choices. It is a theological understanding of what it means to live responsibly in a world where there is evil in every good and good in every evil. Coming to terms with Niebuhr's Christian realism thus requires us both to see how our world is different from the one in which he lived and to ask how his theologically formed way of looking at moral questions might help us understand our own situation. Niebuhr's specific ideas about society and policy may prove useful to us as a point of comparison from which we can see how different our world is, but his understanding of history and human nature illuminate situations that he himself could not have anticipated. We can take the measure of Christian realism for our time by asking what it tells us about three things, in particular: (1) global order in a world that is no longer structured by superpower rivalries; (2) hope and the possibilities for social justice; and (3) the perennial relationship between faith and politics.

Global Order

For more than forty years, from the first Soviet atom bomb test in 1949 to the breakup of the Warsaw Pact in 1991, world affairs were dominated by military and political competition between the United States and the Soviet Union. Events were shaped not only by the ever-present danger of nuclear warfare, but by a technological and cultural competition that shaped the relations of the superpowers with all other nations, as well as with each other. The images of Vice President Richard Nixon debating alternative ways of life with Soviet premier Nikita Khrushchev at a trade exhibition in Moscow and of the leaders of both nations narrowly avoiding war over the presence of Soviet missiles in Cuba serve as reminders of the scope of what Americans called the "Cold War."

Reinhold Niebuhr played an important role in shaping the political understanding that guided American strategy during the early years of this confrontation. Political realism dictated a policy of containment, rather than military victory over the growing Soviet power. Niebuhr's warnings about the limits of power helped guide political leaders toward this realistic strategy. Niebuhr's insistence that no historical power is entirely good or entirely evil, provided the basis for a self-restraint that could be confident of its own moral strength without requiring the defeat of its adversary. Most important, Niebuhr understood the Cold War balance of power as a kind of global order, which had precedents in the experience of earlier imperial powers, and which was far from the worst of the available possibilities. [1] He had argued from his very earliest formulations of Christian realism that the approximations of justice that emerge from conflict are likely to be better than those that result from the imposition of ideals. His defense of democracy suggested that a balance of forces in which no power goes unchallenged helps sustain a free society, even if that means managing tense political relationships with a powerful adversary over many years. For Niebuhrian realists, the Cold War was not a temporary conflict to be resolved in victory. It was a reminder of enduring realities in relationships between nations.

Over time, however, this realistic assessment began to be challenged. Despite the growth of Soviet military power and some spectacular achievements in space exploration, Soviet economic development lagged behind the Western democracies. By the 1980s, American strategists began to envision ways of defeating the rival superpower by economic and technological means. Space-based weapons might even neutralize the threat posed by the arsenal of Soviet nuclear missiles. At the same time, moral and religious leaders began to question the balance of power based on "mutually assured destruction" that had so far prevented actual war between the superpowers. *Was it realistic*, critics asked, *to expect that a system based on massive and immediate nuclear retaliation could continue indefinitely without accident or miscalculation? Was it moral*, America's Catholic bishops asked, *to obtain peace by threatening massive nuclear retaliation, if it would be immoral actually to carry out that threat?* [2]

These developments raised questions about Reinhold Niebuhr's way of looking at global order, but before those questions could be fully answered, the order based on superpower confrontation had itself disappeared. The collapse of the Soviet Union rendered old ideas about deterrence and the balance of power between superpowers obsolete. Political forces that had been kept under control by the rival superpowers now emerged in nationalist movements and international terrorist organizations with military resources that cannot easily be brought under effective control of established governments. New cultural and economic forces that grew out of the technological advances of the Cold War have created a global communications culture, and growing multinational corporations are sometimes richer than the nations whose borders they cross. The world at the beginning of the twenty-first century is largely incomprehensible to the political realism that controlled events by managing the balance of power between nations.

Reinhold Niebuhr's realism, however, could do more than analyze a given system of political relations. He also recognized the historical contingency of the system itself. "God's order can never be identified with some specific form of social organization," he wrote. "It is very important to arrive at concepts of justice which draw upon the common experience of mankind and set a restraint upon human self-interest. But it must be recognized that insofar as such principles of justice are given specific historical meaning, they also become touched by historical contingency." [3]

That sense of the contingency of all things within history is central to what Christian realism contributes to political wisdom. Christian realism is not a theological claim that global order depends on balance of power between nations, forever and ever, world without end. A biblical understanding of history, in fact, should make us alert to the possibility that things may change, requiring us to imagine a wider range of possibilities for organizing a global order. To be realistic, we have to prepare ourselves for a world in which things are far less predictable than they were during the last century, perhaps less predictable than they have been for the last four or five centuries. Cultural forces, economic powers, and religious movements will emerge and dominate events with a speed to which governments have not yet adjusted. It is becoming clear that part of our unpreparedness for the events of September 11 was the simple failure of governments to take seriously the idea that a global terrorist network fired by religious motivations could be anything more than a recurrent nuisance. Nor have we yet begun to create an effective global response to AIDS and other pandemic diseases. No superpowers are likely to arise to solve these problems by coordinating the efforts of governments. We will have to imagine a whole new set of institutions through which powers and interests that have previously been thought of as private can be held accountable to the public good, conceived now on a global scale.

If there are new superpowers, they bear the names of institutions and systems, not nations. Christian realism today must pay attention to the balance of power between economic, cultural, and religious superpowers set alongside the enduring, but now more limited, power of governments. These forces contend to shape the future, just as superpower nations once did.

Niebuhr suggested that it would be better if no one state prevailed without opposition. The future of human freedom may now depend on continuing this same sort of balance of power between religion, business, government, and culture, allowing none of them to shape all of life according to a single plan. Christian realism also suggests that this sort of political order is also the best approximation to justice on a global scale as we are likely to get. The practical task for Christian realists, then, is to work to make sure that all of the basic institutions of government, business, religion, and culture are healthy and powerful, but also to make sure that none of them is powerful enough to set the terms for all the rest. We might call this *pluralistic* Christian realism, to distinguish it from Niebuhr's version that concentrated chiefly on the justice and order that states can create.

This sort of thinking, which does not rely on the power of governments to impose solutions and anticipates new systems of cooperation outside of the framework of government policy and international relations, has made Christian realists uncomfortable in the past. They called it "utopian," which meant, of course, that it was unrealistic. There is a distinction, however, between utopian speculation, which tries to get around the hard realities of human nature, and a realist imagination that tries in times of rapid change to explore all the possibilities in historical contingency. There are risks to pluralistic Christian realism, but the greater risk is a realism that attempts to return all questions to the management of superpower nations, for no good reason except that that is the only system for controlling events whose rules we think we know.

Hope

During the last decades of Niebuhr's life, the domestic struggle for civil rights and racial equality vied with the global dynamics of the Cold War for the attention of the American public. Niebuhr had been concerned with racial discrimination since his early days as a pastor in Detroit, and questions of race and power played a prominent role in *Moral Man and Immoral Society*. The persistence of racial divisions, despite general achievements in the areas of economic and social equality, remained the great failure of American justice. [4]

Niebuhr therefore applauded the *Brown v. Board of Education* decisions by which the Supreme Court began to dismantle the structures of legal segregation in 1954, but he saw this as the articulation of a national ideal of justice that still had a long way to go before it could be realized in practice. His enthusiasm for change was tempered by an aging realist's concern that massive resistance could defeat the cause of justice and leave matters worse than they had been before, especially in the South. Events may have moved very slowly from the perspective of activists whose pressure for change moved quickly from the courts to the legislatures to the streets, but they moved faster than Niebuhr expected after a lifetime of observing the glacial pace of changing social realities. [5] For those who carried the struggle beyond the assassination of Martin Luther King Jr. in 1968 and into the years beyond Niebuhr's death in 1971, his Christian realism became a symbol of good intentions that were not translated into action when action would threaten the existing structures of power.

Women theologians developed a criticism of Niebuhr's thought that perhaps posed a more profound challenge to his system as a whole, for it questioned his account of the biblical view of human nature. Christian realism is about those who hold power, and it views human nature from their perspective. Pride may be the sin of those whose power is not challenged by circumstances, and self-giving love may be the impossible ideal for which we have to keep striving; but for women who are cast in social roles that encourage self-giving to the point of self-annihilation, a little pride would go a long way toward empowering their lives and restoring their full humanity. [6]

Together, these feminist theologians and activists in social justice causes make a potentially devastating critique of Reinhold Niebuhr's Christian realism, because it strikes at the connection between realism and action that was central to Niebuhr's own work and life. Beginning with *An Interpretation of Christian Ethics*, Niebuhr claimed that the point of prophetic faith is to sustain moral action against the forces that lead to complacency or despair. [7] A realistic view of human nature and social structures is an antidote to complacency, which cuts the nerve of action with a sentimental affirmation of things as they are, but that same realism always threatens to lead to despair by presenting obstacles that make change seem impossible. Niebuhr himself understood the threat of despair very well, and the relentless energy that drove his activity at the height of his career seemed sometimes to be a psychological response to the weight of difficulties for which his realism had no completely adequate answer. Despite Niebuhr's own energy and commitment, however, his critics argue that at crucial points in the movement toward racial and gender equality, a complacent version of Christian realism accepted the realities of existing power and left those who most needed justice in despair of ever achieving it. When the attack on racial inequality became intense, the realists cautioned those who were seeking justice against pushing for too much change too fast.

When women began to claim their own roles in church and society, they found the account of human nature that was central to the realists' understanding of politics and society unable to accommodate their experience.

Moving from immediate questions of policy to more basic principles helps redeem Christian realism as an instrument of justice today, just as getting beyond the limitations of Cold War politics helps us understand new possibilities for global order. Some recent interpreters of African American, womanist, and feminist ethics have found resources in Niebuhr's understanding of sin and his analyses of power for taking steps that Niebuhr himself failed to take. [8]

Nevertheless, the criticisms have a point that any future Christian realism must consider. Only, we must be careful how we formulate what that point is. It is not that Christian realism resists change. Most Christian realists wanted to support the revolutions that others were initiating around them in the 1960s and beyond. The problem was not with what they wanted, but with what they expected, and their low expectations derived in large part from the fact that they analyzed the situation without consulting those new voices who might have brought the realists' own presuppositions and limitations into sharper focus. [9] Christian realists supported justice. They did not always listen to women, African Americans, and others who were seeking new conditions for their own lives.

As a result, traditional Christian realism often lacks the element of hope that can only be provided by those who view events from outside the centers of power and security. Hope is not the same thing as the sentimental optimism about human nature that the realists rejected, nor is it the confidence of Social Gospel theologians that progress would surely follow from existing historical conditions, if only knowledge and moral conviction could be appropriately joined by Christian love. Hope is not an estimate that change is likely, but the awareness that something else is, nonetheless, possible. Hope sustains those who have no stake in the present, even when they have no good reason to expect anything better in the future.

Those whose chances are somewhat better, and who therefore have more to lose, may describe such hope as "eschatological" or "apocalyptic." Like calling alternative ideas about global order "utopian," this is a way of saying that such hopes are unrealistic. There are no grounds for these hopes, the realist warning goes, in the real world where change must be achieved. To this, today's Christian realist must reply that hope is nonetheless a real part of the human situation. Hope is not based on a utopian transformation of human nature or an apocalyptic abolition of governments and institutional structures. Hope is a demand for new institutions that will allow the things people envision as possible for themselves, precisely as the human beings they are, to come into being.

People maintain this hope without reference to realistic possibilities, and any assessment that does not take their hope into account is unrealistic. It will eventually prove false, as unrealistic expectations do. If Christian realism began by pointing out that Social Gospel expectations were too high, a realist with the same principles, looking back over the last third of the twentieth century, would have to say that the assessments of Christian realism sometimes failed because their expectations were too low. On the basis of twentieth-century realism's estimates, the Civil Rights Movement should have stalled out against massive white resistance. The Velvet Revolution at the end of the 1980s should have been crushed like the earlier uprising in Hungary in the 1950s. The Berlin Wall would still be standing, and Nelson Mandela would in all likelihood have died in prison.

Unsentimental realists, of course, would not have wanted any of those outcomes, but their way of understanding the balances of power, the ambiguities of change, and the ironies of history would have led them to expect those results, or something like them. So the question at the beginning of the twenty-first century becomes, "Who is the realist?" Is it those who expect institutional inertia to control the pace of events because self-interested people always prefer present order to uncertain possibilities? Or is it those who hope for changes that would realize the best possibilities they can imagine for themselves?

We might call the latter view *hopeful* Christian realism, borrowing a phrase from Douglas Ottati, [10] to complement the *pluralistic* Christian realism that offers a more expansive view of the possibilities for global order. Hopeful realism recognizes that imagination and creativity are part of human nature, along with the capacity to see things clearly as they are. In a pluralistic world, where governments are not the only bearers of power sufficient to shape political reality, hopeful realism will work to ensure that those who are the bearers of hope become real participants in deliberations about the future. That openness will be more just, but it will also be more realistic. It will be more likely to figure out what is really going to happen, because it will not neglect the power of hope.

From the 1950s through the 1980s, being realistic meant recognizing that nuclear deterrence and the balance of power had created a stable system of relative security, despite idealistic longings for more justice at home and more peace in the world. Paying attention to what was happening meant reminding people of some enduring, if unattractive, features of the human condition and trimming expectations to fit those constraints. Now, those particular structures of stability have largely disappeared, and we may be about to experience cultural change and institutional transformations on a scale unprecedented since the beginning of the modern era. To be a Christian realist in the twenty-first century will mean listening to all the voices and taking all of the possibilities seriously, rather than trying to keep hope and fear within the bounds of existing institutions.

Faith and Politics

New ways of thinking about peace and justice have led Christian realists to rethink some of Reinhold Niebuhr's ideas about global order and political equality, but changes in the world of events have also led to questions about Niebuhr's understanding of the relationship between biblical faith and American life. The development of religious diversity and controversy over the public use of religious symbols make it harder to draw the connections between religion and American life that previous generations could take for granted.

While some are nostalgic for the old forms of public religion, the most important theological critics want to leave those connections behind for good. Today, they say, Christians cannot live in expectation of a widely shared way of life that would also meet the requirements of their faith. They can only offer a witness to religious truth, which has suddenly been made aware of the gap between faithful Christian practice and the way that people in modern, secular society live, even when they are trying to be just, peaceful, and moral.

In recent Christian ethics, Stanley Hauerwas best represents this position of the witness, and he is particularly clear about how his theology shapes a criticism of Christian realism. The problem is "Constantinianism." "Put simply," Hauerwas says, "Constantinianism is the attempt to make Christianity necessary, to make the church at home in the world, in a manner that witness is no longer required."[11] As the name suggests, the problem predates modern democracy, but it is not the Emperor Constantine's conversion that troubles Hauerwas. It is the Constantinian assumption that Christianity can be made "necessary" to the wider society, that it can be "at home in the world."

What, then, does a church that is not at home in the world do? The short answer is that it lives its faith in community as a witness to the world. "The first task of Christian social ethics," for Hauerwas, "is not to make the 'world' better or more just, but to help Christian people form their community consistent with their conviction that the story of Christ is a truthful account of our existence."[12] Becoming that kind of community is not a preliminary exercise before tackling the questions of justice and peace in the world. Becoming that kind of community is the most that Christians can accomplish. Witness is not an exhortation to the wider society, urging it to become more moral, more just, or more like the Christian community, as though such a thing were possible. Witness is the integrity of the church's claim to be what it is.

As Hauerwas sees it, it is risky to take witness beyond this point. We should not even try to talk about good and evil, better and worse, more and less justice in terms that society can understand. It is unwise, and indeed impossible, to provide a rational validation of Christian truth apart from the Christian narrative. It is not a matter of learning from experience when to try to speak to the world and when not to. Efforts to communicate a narrated truth in terms that go beyond its narrative context never work.

From this perspective, of course, the whole project of Christian realism, especially the way that Reinhold Niebuhr presents it, must be judged a distortion of the Christian message. "Niebuhr's work now represents the worst of two worlds: most secular people do not find his arguments convincing; yet his theology is not sufficient to provide the means for Christians to sustain their lives. . . . Niebuhr's theology reflects the loss of truthful Christian speech and, hence, of faithful Christian practice." [13]

Hauerwas has forcefully brought American Christians to confront some important recent changes in the public role of religion. It is now less easy than it sometimes was for Reinhold Niebuhr, John Courtney Murray, and Robert Gordis to suggest that Americans share a single, unified moral and political tradition that is grounded in biblical ideas of creation and natural law. This fragmentation of our moral and religious perspectives is widely discussed, and its implications are contested. Hauerwas thinks that Christians should develop their witness apart from public, political discussions, and some philosophers suggest that religious voices should be excluded from public forums unless they are prepared to offer "public reasons" for the policies they advocate. [14] Other recent writers, notably Jeffrey Stout, suggest that Augustinian Christian faith and Emersonian American democracy might have something important to say to one another, [15] but even those who encourage the dialogue are now likely to recognize that the religious and political traditions involved are diverse in origin, multiple, and significantly different from one another.

Is Hauerwas right, then, that Niebuhr's realism simply offers us the worst of both worlds? Probably not. Niebuhr's understanding of the relationship between prophetic faith and democratic practice was complex—more complex than his own statements sometimes make it, and certainly more complex than Hauerwas takes it to be. Prophetic faith brings an "impossible ideal" to bear on all the approximations of justice that a society has to offer at any particular time. The biblical idea that every human being is both made in the image of God and is an anxious, self-interested, and sinful creature plays out in history and politics as well as in individual lives. It also plays out in churches. The continuity between the community of faith and the political community is greater for Niebuhr than it seems to be for Hauerwas, precisely because Christians participate in both of them.

In the Niebuhrian understanding of human nature and moral judgments that we have traced through this book, human freedom and creativity generate real prospects for improvement in lives and societies. We can make responsible decisions that result in more justice, rather than less. We can extend our moral concern to a wider community, rather than reducing it to a smaller, self-interested one, even if we never achieve the impossible ideal of universal love. At the same time, each advance in love and justice creates possibilities for idolatry, for treating progress as more complete and final than it really is. Each step forward generates its own potential for ironic reversals that leave us with new and unforeseen problems. Prophetic faith provides a steady reminder of both the risks and the possibilities. [16]

The result of this theological understanding, which is set out primarily in Niebuhr's early work from *An Interpretation of Christian Ethics* through *The Nature and Destiny of Man*, becomes more explicit in the later political writings and occasional essays. "There is no 'Christian' economic or political system.... God's order can never be identified with some specific form of social organization." [17] Christian faith both illuminates both prophetic possibilities and shines the light of prophetic judgment on every political choice. For that reason, too, there can be no single, simple theological judgment about history and politics in general.

Hauerwas is right about the dangers of idolatry when a nation or a society thinks too highly of its own virtue. He is wrong to think that this is the only message of prophetic faith. From Reinhold Niebuhr, we learn that both idolatry and justice are possible, and we are set to the task of making discriminating judgments between them. We learn that human freedom gives us possibilities that cannot be confined by order and also that self-interest will distort every idea of what justice requires from us or requires for our neighbors. From the realists of Niebuhr's generation, we have learned the lessons about idolatry and self-interest well. If Hauerwas' work is any indication, some of Niebuhr's most severe critics have been his best pupils in those lessons.

The question for the future is whether we can now create a hopeful, pluralistic Christian realism that will bring prophetic faith to bear in a new way on the very different realities that shape the world today. If we do that, we will not always say exactly what Reinhold Niebuhr said, but we will be doing what he did. He paid attention to what was really happening, and he looked at events with a wisdom shaped by a biblical understanding of history and human nature. This did not give him access to unambiguous truths or provide him with blueprints for justice that need never be revised, but it did enable him to describe new conditions in terms that made sense to many people. A Christian witness in social and political life may need to do more than that, but we cannot settle for less.

Questions for Reflection

1. How has the end of the Cold War changed the problems of maintaining peace and global order? Does Niebuhr's emphasis on balance of power still provide guidance in this new situation?

2. What led activists concerned about racial and gender justice to criticize Niebuhr's Christian realism? How might Christian realism provide the hope that is necessary to sustain these movements for greater justice?

3. What do critics of Christian realism mean when they say that realism is a version of "Constantinianism"? To what extent does Niebuhr believe that a Christian realist must take responsibility for society?

NOTES

Introduction

1. This phrase from 2 Corinthians 6:8 was a favorite of Niebuhr's, and he used it as the title of one of his best sermons on the possibilities and limitations of theology. See Reinhold Niebuhr, *Beyond Tragedy* (New York: Charles Scribner's Sons, 1937), 3–24.

2. Reinhold Niebuhr, *An Interpretation of Christian Ethics* (New York: Seabury Press, 1979), 64.

3. See Martin Halliwell, *The Constant Dialogue: Reinhold Niebuhr and American Intellectual Culture* (Lanham, Md.: Rowman & Littlefield, 2005).

4. Reinhold earned a B.D. and an M.A. from Yale. H. Richard, the more academic of the two, completed his Ph.D., served as president of Elmhurst College, and eventually returned to Yale as a member of the faculty.

5. Reinhold Niebuhr, *Leaves from the Notebook of a Tamed Cynic* (Louisville: Westminster John Knox Press, 1990).

6. Reinhold Niebuhr, *Moral Man and Immoral Society* (Louisville: Westminster John Knox Press, 2001).

7. Niebuhr, *An Interpretation of Christian Ethics*, 62.

8. Reinhold Niebuhr, *The Nature and Destiny of Man*, 2 vols. (Louisville: Westminster John Knox Press, 1996).

9. Richard Fox, *Reinhold Niebuhr: A Biography* (Ithaca: Cornell University Press, 1996), 191.

10. Niebuhr, *Nature and Destiny*, vol. 1, 16.

11. Reinhold Niebuhr, *Faith and Politics*, ed. Ronald Stone (New York: George Braziller, 1968), 56.

12. Reinhold Niebuhr, *The Structure of Nations and Empires* (New York: Charles Scribner's Sons, 1959).

13. For an account of Niebuhr's life and work in these years, see especially the memoir written by his daughter, Elisabeth Sifton, *The Serenity Prayer: Faith and Politics in Times of Peace and War* (New York: Norton, 2003).

1. Immoral Society

1. Niebuhr, *Leaves from the Notebook of a Tamed Cynic* (Louisville: Westminster John Knox Press, 1990), 42–43. See Fox, *Reinhold Niebuhr: A Biography* (Ithaca: Cornell University Press, 1996), 77–80.

2. Barth announced his theological program in 1921 with a commentary on Paul's letter to the Romans. See Karl Barth, *The Epistle to the Romans* (New York: Oxford University Press, 1968).

3. See Reinhold Niebuhr, *Essays in Applied Christianity*, ed. D. B. Robertson (New York: Meridian Books, 1959), 141–47.

4. Charles M. Sheldon, *In His Steps* (New York: Barnes and Noble, 2004), 11–16.

5. Walter Rauschenbusch, *Christianity and the Social Crisis* (New York: Macmillan, 1907), 421.

6. Walter Rauschenbusch, *A Theology for the Social Gospel* (New York: Macmillan, 1917), 4.

7. Niebuhr, *Moral Man and Immoral Society* (Lousiville: Westminster John Knox Press, 1932), 129.

8. Ibid., 253.

9. Martin Luther King Jr., "Letter from Birmingham City Jail," in *A Testament of Hope: The Essential Writings and Speeches of Martin Luther King, Jr.*, ed. James M. Washington (San Francisco: HarperSanFrancisco, 1991), 292.

10. Reinhold Niebuhr, "When Will Christians Stop Fooling Themselves?" in *Love and Justice: Selections from the Shorter Writings of Reinhold Niebuhr*, ed. D. B. Robertson (Louisville: Westminster John Knox Press, 1992), 43.

11. Niebuhr, *Moral Man and Immoral Society*, 113–68.

12. Lee Cormie, "The Hermeneutical Privilege of the Oppressed," *Catholic Theological Society of America Proceedings* 33 (1978): 78.

13. Niebuhr, *Moral Man and Immoral Society*, 277.

14. Ibid., 259.

15. H. Richard Niebuhr, "The Grace of Doing Nothing," *Christian Century* 49 (March 23, 1932): 378–80.

16. Reinhold Niebuhr, *Reflections on the End of an Era* (New York: Charles Scribner's Sons, 1934), 224.

17. On Niebuhr's life during the early 1930s, see Fox, *Reinhold Niebuhr*, 121–41; and Charles C. Brown, *Niebuhr and His Age: Reinhold Niebuhr's Prophetic*

Role in the Twentieth Century (Philadelphia: Trinity Press International, 1992), 36–53.

18. Niebuhr, *Faith and Politics*, ed. Ronald Stone (New York: George Braziller, 1968), 56.

19. Niebuhr, *An Interpretation of Christian Ethics* (New York: Seabury Press, 1979), 63.

20. Ibid., 35.

21. Ibid., 63.

22. Ibid., 84–102.

23. Ibid., 23–24.

24. W. A. Visser 't Hooft and J. H. Oldham, *The Church and Its Function in Society* (Chicago: Willett, Clark & Co., 1937), 194.

25. William Temple, *Christianity and the Social Order* (New York: Penguin Books, 1942), 56–62. Emil Brunner, *The Divine Imperative* (Philadelphia: Westminster Press, 1948).

26. Niebuhr, *Nature and Destiny*, vol. 1 (Louisville: Westminster John Knox Press, 1996), 1.

27. See Ibid., vol. 2, 213–43.

2. Human Nature

1. Niebuhr, *An Interpretation of Christian Ethics* (New York: Seabury Press, 1979), 1–21.

2. Karl Barth, *The Holy Spirit and the Christian Life* (Louisville: Westminster John Knox Press, 1993), 9.

3. Niebuhr's intent sometimes seems even more universal. His writings include occasional references to Buddhist ideas about human nature and comparisons with the "logic of non-historical cultures in the oriental world," but these often lack the detailed knowledge of texts and nuanced comparisons that mark his discussions of Western thought. See, for example, *Nature and Destiny*, vol. 1, 125; vol. 2, 13–14.

4. "History of the Gifford Lectures"; available from http://www.giffordlec tures.org/online.asp; Internet; accessed 7 July 2006.

5. Niebuhr, *Nature and Destiny*, vol. 1, 1–25. As noted in the introduction, Niebuhr delivered his Gifford Lectures in two series. The first series, on "human nature," was revised and published in 1941. The second, on "human destiny," appeared in 1943. In 1946, with both series available, the publisher, Charles Scribner's Sons, combined them into a single volume. This proved unwieldy, and the two-volume edition returned in 1964. All publications of the two-volume edition have the same pagination, so the references to volume and page number

in this book (e.g., vol. 1, 13) should fit most versions of *Nature and Destiny* that the reader may find available.

6. Niebuhr, *Nature and Destiny*, vol. 1, 16.

7. Ibid., vol. 2, 74.

8. Plato, *The Republic*, 7.514b-520a.

9. Niebuhr, *Nature and Destiny*, vol. 1, 12.

10. Langdon Gilkey, *On Niebuhr: A Theological Study* (Chicago: University of Chicago Press, 2001), 104.

11. Niebuhr, *Nature and Destiny*, vol. 1, 182.

12. Gilkey, *On Niebuhr: A Theological Study*, 104.

13. Late in his career, after considerable reading in contemporary psychology, Niebuhr wrote more directly about the connection between these different levels on which human nature expresses itself in *The Self and the Dramas of History* (New York: Charles Scribner's Sons, 1955).

14. Niebuhr, *Nature and Destiny*, vol. 1, 186.

15. Ibid., 207.

16. The seven deadly sins are: pride, avarice, lust, gluttony, anger, envy, and sloth.

17. Niebuhr, *Nature and Destiny*, vol. 1, 178–79.

18. Ibid., 150.

19. Niebuhr, *An Interpretation of Christian Ethics*, 16.

20. Niebuhr, *Nature and Destiny*, vol. 1, 241–64.

21. See chapter 1, note 15.

22. Niebuhr, *Nature and Destiny*, vol. 1, 219–27.

23. Ibid., 222.

24. Roy Jenkins, *Churchill* (New York: Farrar, Straus, and Giroux, 2001), 589–610.

3. Human Destiny

1. Reinhold Niebuhr, *Faith and History* (New York: Charles Scribner's Sons, 1949), 152.

2. H. Richard Niebuhr provides an important summary of this American understanding of Jesus in *The Kingdom of God in America* (New York: Harper and Brothers, 1937), 88–126.

3. Niebuhr, *An Interpretation of Christian Ethics* (New York: Seabury Press, 1979), 65.

4. Niebuhr, *Nature and Destiny* (Louisville: Westminster John Knox Press, 1996), vol. 2, 1–34.

5. See Acts 1:6-8.

6. See chapter 2, note 18.

7. Niebuhr, *An Interpretation of Christian Ethics*, 22–23.

8. Niebuhr, *Nature and Destiny*, vol. 1, 12.

9. Ibid., 10–12.

10. Niebuhr builds this understanding of tragedy on an interpretation of Friedrich Nietzsche. See *Nature and Destiny*, vol. 1, 11.

11. Niebuhr, *Faith and History*, 151.

12. See Eugene TeSelle, *Augustine* (Nashville: Abingdon Press, 2006), 62–63.

13. Oliver O'Donovan, *Common Objects of Love* (Grand Rapids: Eerdmans, 2002), 41. See also O'Donovan, *The Ways of Judgment* (Grand Rapids: Eerdmans, 2005), 28–30.

14. Niebuhr, *Nature and Destiny*, vol. 2, 246.

15. Niebuhr, *Faith and Politics*, 53.

16. Niebuhr, *Christian Realism and Political Problems* (New York: Charles Scribner's Sons, 1953), 14; "The Negro Minority and Its Fate in a Self-Righteous Nation," *Social Action* 35 (October, 1968): 53–64.

17. Niebuhr, *Faith and Politics*, 56.

18. Niebuhr, *Love and Justice*, 58.

19. Reinhold Niebuhr, *The Irony of American History* (New York: Charles Scribner's Sons, 1952).

20. Niebuhr, *An Interpretation of Christian Ethics*, 64.

21. Niebuhr, *Nature and Destiny*, vol. 2, 43.

22. Utilitarian moral philosophy shows that these calculations can cover a very wide range of human activity, and the demands they generate can sometimes be quite rigorous.

23. Niebuhr, *Nature and Destiny*, vol. 2, 15.

24. Niebuhr, *Faith and History*, 152.

4. Democracy

1. Reinhold Niebuhr, *Love and Justice: Selections from the Shorter Writings of Reinhold Niebuhr*, ed. D. B. Robertson (Louisville: Westminster John Knox Press, 1992), 43. See chapter 1, note 10.

2. Reinhold Niebuhr, *The Children of Light and the Children of Darkness* (New York: Charles Scribner's Sons, 1944), 16–17.

3. Ibid., 9.

4. Ibid.

5. See chapter 3, note 11. For similar ideas, see *The Children of Light and the Children of Darkness*, 3–4, 39.

6. Niebuhr, *The Children of Light and the Children of Darkness*, 10.

7. See chapter 3, note 9.

8. Niebuhr, *The Children of Light and the Children of Darkness*, 32–33.

9. Of course, according to the Marxists, once this happens, there will be no more self-interest and thus no need of a higher law to limit it. Niebuhr criticizes the "utopianism" of this view of history in more detail later in *The Children of Light and the Children of Darkness*, 106–17.

10. The political philosopher John Rawls suggested this sort of understanding of democracy in *The Law of Peoples* (Cambridge, Mass.: Harvard University Press, 1999).

11. Niebuhr, *The Children of Light and the Children of Darkness*, 11.

12. Ibid., 7.

13. Martin Luther, "Temporal Authority: To What Extent It Should Be Obeyed," in *Martin Luther's Basic Theological Writings*, ed. Timothy F. Lull (Minneapolis: Fortress Press, 1989), 666.

14. Augustine, *The City of God against the Pagans*, ed. R. W. Dyson (Cambridge: Cambridge University Press, 1998), 926–28; Luther, "Temporal Authority," 669.

15. See Reinhold Niebuhr, "Why the Christian Church Is Not Pacifist," in *Christianity and Power Politics* (New York: Charles Scribner's Sons, 1940), 1–32.

16. Reinhold Niebuhr, "Greek Tragedy and Modern Politics," in *Christianity and Power Politics* (Hamden, Conn.: Archon Books, 1969), 104.

17. Ibid.

18. Niebuhr, *The Children of Light and the Children of Darkness*, xiii.

5. Faith and History

1. See, for example, Morton White, *Social Thought in America: The Revolt against Formalism* (Boston: Beacon Press, 1957), 247–64.

2. Reinhold Niebuhr, *Faith and History* (New York: Charles Scribner's Sons, 1949).

3. Barth, born in 1886, was slightly older than Niebuhr and died in 1968, three years before Niebuhr.

4. Reinhold Niebuhr, "We Are Men and Not God," in *Essays in Applied Christianity*, ed. D. B. Robertson (New York: Meridian Books, 1959), 172.

5. Emil Brunner, *The Divine Imperative*, trans. Olive Wyon (Philadelphia: Westminster Press, 1947).

6. Charles E. Curran and Richard A. McCormick, *Natural Law and Theology* (New York: Paulist Press, 1991).

7. Niebuhr, *Nature and Destiny* (Louisville: Westminster John Knox Press, 1996), vol. 1, 281.

8. John Courtney Murray, *We Hold These Truths: Catholic Reflections on the American Proposition* (New York: Sheed and Ward, 1960), 97–123.

9. Robert Gordis, *The Root and the Branch: Judaism and the Free Society* (Chicago: University of Chicago Press, 1962).

10. See J. Leon Hooper, *The Ethics of Discourse: The Social Philosophy of John Courtney Murray* (Washington, D.C.: Georgetown University Press, 1986).

11. For a complete study of the intellectual relations between Murray and Niebuhr, including their discussions of natural law, see Thomas C. Berg, "John Courtney Murray and Reinhold Niebuhr: Natural Law and Christian Realism," *Journal of Catholic Social Thought* 4 (Winter 2007): 3–28.

12. Murray, *We Hold These Truths*, 282.

13. Ibid.

14. Niebuhr, *Faith and Politics*, ed. Ronald Stone (New York: George Braziller, 1968), 198.

15. See Paul Ramsey, *Nine Modern Moralists* (Englewood Cliffs, N.J.: Prentice-Hall, 1962), 111–31.

16. Niebuhr, *Faith and History*, 171–95.

17. Joseph Bernardin, *A Consistent Ethic of Life* (Kansas City, Mo.: Sheed and Ward, 1988).

18. See Charles Curran, *The Catholic Moral Tradition Today* (Washington, D.C.: Georgetown University Press, 1999), 40–42.

19. For a review of the churches' role in creating the Universal Declaration of Human Rights, see John S. Nurser, *For All Peoples and Nations: The Ecumenical Church and Human Rights* (Washington, D.C.: Georgetown University Press, 2005).

20. Charles W. Kegley and Robert W. Bretall, eds., *Reinhold Niebuhr: His Religious, Social, and Political Thought.* Library of Living Theology. (New York: Macmillan, 1961).

21. Reinhold Niebuhr, "Coherence, Incoherence, and Christian Faith," in *Christian Realism and Political Problems* (New York: Charles Scribner's Sons, 1953), 175–203.

22. White, *Social Thought in America*, 257.

23. Niebuhr, *Faith and History*, 152.

6. Christian Realism: Pluralistic and Hopeful

1. Reinhold Niebuhr, *The Structure of Nations and Empires* (New York: Charles Scribner's Sons, 1959).

2. National Conference of Catholic Bishops, *The Challenge of Peace: God's Promise and Our Response* (Washington, D.C.: United States Catholic Conference, 1983).

3. Reinhold Niebuhr, *Faith and Politics*, ed. Ronald Stone (New York: George Braziller, 1968), 105.

4. Ibid., 197.

5. Charles Marsh, *The Beloved Community: How Faith Shapes Social Justice from the Civil Rights Movement to Today* (New York: Basic Books, 2005), 39–41.

6. Daphne Hampson, "Reinhold Niebuhr on Sin: A Critique," in *Reinhold Niebuhr and the Issues of Our Time*, ed. Richard Harries (Grand Rapids: Eerdmans, 1986), 46–60.

7. Niebuhr, *An Interpretation of Christian Ethics* (New York: Seabury Press, 1979), 62–70.

8. See, for example, Rebekah Miles, *Bonds of Freedom: Feminist Theology and Christian Realism* (New York: Oxford University Press, 2001); Mary McClintock Fulkerson, *Places of Redemption: Theology for a Worldly Church* (Oxford: Oxford University Press, 2007).

9. Traci West points this out with particular acuteness by comparing Niebuhr's realism with events that were happening in Harlem, just a short distance from Union Theological Seminary, as early as the 1930s. See Traci C. West, *Disruptive Christian Ethics: When Racism and Women's Lives Matter* (Louisville: Westminster John Knox Press, 2006), 3–35.

10. Douglas F. Ottati, *Hopeful Realism: Reclaiming the Poetry of Theology* (Cleveland: Pilgrim Press, 1999).

11. Stanley Hauerwas, *With the Grain of the Universe: The Church's Witness and Natural Theology* (Grand Rapids: Brazos Press, 2001), 221.

12. Stanley Hauerwas, *A Community of Character* (Notre Dame, Ind.: University of Notre Dame Press, 1981), 10.

13. Hauerwas, *With the Grain of the Universe*, 139–40.

14. See, for example, the discussion in Robert Audi and Nicholas Wolterstorff, *Religion in the Public Square: The Place of Religious Convictions in Political Debate* (Lanham, Md.: Rowman and Littlefield, 1997).

15. Jeffrey Stout, *Democracy and Tradition* (Princeton: Princeton University Press, 2004).

16. Niebuhr, *An Interpretation of Christian Ethics*, 64.

17. Niebuhr, *Faith and Politics*, 56, 105.

SELECTED BIBLIOGRAPHY

T his bibliography includes major works by Niebuhr, important collections of essays and incidental writings, and studies of Niebuhr and Christian realism written by Niebuhr's contemporaries and later authors. It should provide an up-to-date starting point for further study, but it is by no means complete. For further resources on Niebuhr and his work, see the two comprehensive bibliographies listed at the end.

Major Works and Collections of Reinhold Niebuhr

[1932] *Moral Man and Immoral Society: A Study in Ethics and Politics*. Louisville: Westminster John Knox Press, 2001.

[1935] *An Interpretation of Christian Ethics*. New York: Seabury Press, 1979.

[1938] *Beyond Tragedy*. New York: Charles Scribner's Sons.

[1941, 1943] *The Nature and Destiny of Man*, 2 vols. Louisville: Westminster John Knox Press, 1996.

[1944] *The Children of Light and the Children of Darkness: A Vindication of Democracy and a Critique of Its Traditional Defence*. New York: Charles Scribner's Sons, 1972.

[1949] *Faith and History: A Comparison of Christian and Modern Views of History*. New York: Charles Scribner's Sons.

[1952] *The Irony of American History*. New York: Charles Scribner's Sons.

[1953] *Christian Realism and Political Problems*. New York: Charles Scribner's Sons.

[1955] *The Self and the Dramas of History*. New York: Charles Scribner's Sons.

[1957] *Love and Justice: Selections from the Shorter Writings of Reinhold Niebuhr*. D. B. Robertson, ed. Louisville: Westminster John Knox Press, 1992.

[1958] *Pious and Secular America*. New York: Charles Scribner's Sons.

[1959] *Essays in Applied Christianity*. D. B. Robertson, ed. Cleveland: World Publishing.

[1959] *The Structure of Nations and Empires*. New York: Charles Scribner's Sons.

[1968] *Faith and Politics*. Ronald Stone, ed. New York: George Braziller.

Secondary Sources on Reinhold Niebuhr

Bingham, June. *Courage to Change: An Introduction to the Life and Thought of Reinhold Niebuhr*. New York: Charles Scribner's Sons, 1961.

Brown, Charles C. *Niebuhr and His Age: Reinhold Niebuhr's Prophetic Role and Legacy*. New ed. Harrisburg: Trinity Press International, 2002.

Brown, Robert McAfee, ed. *The Essential Reinhold Niebuhr: Selected Essays and Addresses*. New Haven: Yale University Press, 1986.

Clark, Henry B. *Serenity, Courage, and Wisdom: The Enduring Legacy of Reinhold Niebuhr*. Cleveland: Pilgrim Press, 1994.

Fackre, Gabriel. *The Promise of Reinhold Niebuhr*. Lanham, Md.: University Press of America, 1994.

———. "Was Reinhold Niebuhr a Christian?" *First Things* 126 (October 2002): 25–27.

Fox, Richard Wightman. *Reinhold Niebuhr: A Biography*. Ithaca: Cornell University Press, 1996.

———. "The Niebuhr Brothers and the Liberal Protestant Heritage," in Michael J. Lacy, ed. *Religion and Twentieth-Century American Intellectual Life*. Cambridge: Cambridge University Press, 1991.

Gilkey, Langdon. *On Niebuhr: A Theological Study*. Chicago: University of Chicago Press, 2001.

———. "Reinhold Niebuhr's Theology of History." *Journal of Religion* 54 (October 1974): 360–86.

Halliwell, Martin. *The Constant Dialogue: Reinhold Niebuhr and American Intellectual Culture*. Lanham, Md.: Rowman & Littlefield, 2005.

Harland, Gordon. *The Thought of Reinhold Niebuhr*. New York: Oxford University Press, 1960.

Harries, Richard, ed. *Reinhold Niebuhr and the Issues of Our Time*. London: Mowbray, 1986.

Kamergrauzis, Normunds. *The Persistence of Christian Realism: A Study in the Social Ethics of Ronald H. Preston*. Uppsala, Sweden: Uppsala University Library, 2001.

Kegley, Charles W. and Robert W. Bretall, eds. *Reinhold Niebuhr: His Religious, Social, and Political Thought*. The Library of Living Theology. New York: Macmillan, 1956.

Lindbeck, George. "Revelation, Natural Law, and the Thought of Reinhold Niebuhr." *Natural Law Forum* 4 (1959): 146–51.

Lovin, Robin. *Reinhold Niebuhr and Christian Realism.* Cambridge: Cambridge University Press, 1995.

———. "Reinhold Niebuhr in Contemporary Scholarship: A Review Essay." *Journal of Religious Ethics* 31 (Winter 2003): 489–505.

Macgregor, G. H. C. *The Relevance of the Impossible: A Reply to Reinhold Niebuhr.* London: The Fellowship of Reconciliation, 1941.

McKeogh, Colm. *The Political Realism of Reinhold Niebuhr: A Pragmatic Approach to Just War.* New York: St. Martin's Press, 1997.

Niebuhr, Ursula, ed. *Remembering Reinhold Niebuhr: Letters of Reinhold and Ursula Niebuhr.* New York: HarperCollins, 1991.

Rice, Daniel F. *Reinhold Niebuhr and John Dewey: An American Odyssey.* Albany: SUNY Press, 1993.

Scott, Nathan A., ed. *The Legacy of Reinhold Niebuhr.* Chicago: University of Chicago Press, 1975.

Sifton, Elisabeth. *The Serenity Prayer: Faith and Politics in Times of Peace and War.* New York: Norton, 2003.

Stone, Ronald H. *Professor Reinhold Niebuhr: A Mentor to the Twentieth Century.* Louisville: Westminster John Knox Press, 1992.

Warren, Heather A. *Theologians of a New World Order: Reinhold Niebuhr and the Christian Realists 1920–1948.* New York: Oxford University Press, 1997.

Other Resources and Studies of Christian Realism

Bennett, John C. *Christian Realism.* London: Student Christian Movement Press, 1941.

Dorrien, Gary. *Soul and Society: The Making and Renewing of Social Christianity.* Minneapolis: Fortress Press, 1995.

———. *Idealism, Realism, and Modernity, 1900–1950. The Making of American Liberal Theology.* Louisville: Westminster John Knox Press, 2003.

Hauerwas, Stanley. *With the Grain of the Universe.* Grand Rapids: Brazos Press, 2001.

Horton, Walter Marshall. *Realistic Theology.* New York: Harper, 1934.

Macintosh, Douglas Clyde. *Religious Realism.* New York: Macmillan, 1931.

Meyer, Donald B. *The Protestant Search for Political Realism, 1919–1941.* Los Angeles: University of California Press, 1960.

Ottati, Douglas. *Hopeful Realism.* Cleveland: Pilgrim Press, 1989.

West, Charles C. *Communism and the Theologians: Study of an Encounter.* London: SCM Press, 1958.

West, Cornel. *The American Evasion of Philosophy: A Geneaology of Pragmatism.* Madison: University of Wisconsin, 1989.

————. *Democracy Matters*. New York: Penguin Press, 2004.

Bibliographical Resources

Brown, Charles C. *Niebuhr and His Age: Reinhold Niebuhr's Prophetic Role and Legacy*. New ed. Harrisburg, Pa.: Trinity Press International, 2002.
This new edition has a significant bibliography, including new publications of Niebuhr's works and new secondary sources.

Robertson, D. B. *Reinhold Niebuhr's Works: A Bibliography*. Lanham, Md.: University Press of America, 1983.
This is the definitive bibliography of Reinhold Niebuhr's works, with a significant listing of secondary sources through 1983.

INDEX OF NAMES

Index of Subjects